OPERATION SKY-DROP!

Action Man grabbed G.I. Joe's arm and pulled the American to the ground. He had seen a lick of flame spurt out from the engine of the first truck to turn over.

Almost before they hit the earth a tremendous flash of fire shot high into the air followed by an explosion and shock-wave which lifted them bodily and crashed them down again. More explosions followed, deafening.

They rose to their knees, peering down into the hollow. They could see at least a dozen tanks among the trees, all of them sitting in a sea of blazing petrol . . .

3 cde

Other ACTION MAN books

HOLD THE BRIDGE
SNOW, ICE AND BULLETS
THE TAKING OF MONTE CARRILLO

All published by CORGI CAROUSEL BOOKS LTD.

OPERATION SKY-DROP

MIKE BROGAN

CORGI CAROUSEL BOOKS LTD
A DIVISION OF TRANSWORLD PUBLISHERS LTD

OPERATION SKY-DROP
A CORGI CAROUSEL BOOK 0 552 52076 4

Originally published in Great Britain by
Aidan Ellis Ltd.

PRINTING HISTORY
Aidan Ellis edition published 1977
Corgi Carousel edition published 1977

Carousel Books are published by
Transworld Publishers Ltd.,
Century House, 61–63 Uxbridge Road,
Ealing, London W5 5SA
Made and printed in Great Britain by
Cox & Wyman Ltd., London, Reading and Fakenham

CONTENTS

OPERATION SKY-DROP

CHAPTER ONE

IN THE WRONG PLACE!

Action Man, piloting the Horsa glider, gently eased the controls to allow the craft to swing back until it was lined up with the tail of the Stirling bomber ahead. The tow line connecting the two aircraft sagged slightly between them. Torn rags of cloud drifted past, cloud that had in the past twenty minutes become more and more dense.

The Stirling pilot's voice crackled over the inter-com. "Ten minutes to target, Action Man. You okay back there? You can expect flak to be thrown up at you from now on."

Somewhere off to the starboard side of the glider flew the rest of the vast air armada, taking more than three thousand men of the Airborne Division to the dropping zone in Germany. But the C-47's with their paratroops, and the Stirlings and Halifaxs towing their gliders, which had been clearly visible when they had taken off into the blue sky above England were now hidden in the increasing cloud cover.

Beside Action Man in the co-pilot's seat, G.I. Joe had been reading a newspaper, as though he were a businessman on the way to the office rather than a soldier about to be plunged into battle behind enemy lines. Now he put the paper away and said: "Ten minutes, eh, buddy-boy?" He nodded at the windshield ahead of them where the cloud, thickening rapidly, almost hid the Stirling from view. "Let's hope the guy in front knows the way." Then he added almost as an afterthought: "Flak coming up now. Lots of it."

Action Man turned to look back at the cabin behind which twenty-five highly-trained fighting men, bulky with their equipment, sat talking quietly among themselves.

"Be a bit noisy from now on, lads!" he called. "Jerry's popping off. Seven minutes from the dropping zone, so stand by."

In the cockpit of the glider it seemed as though lights were being switched on and off, red lights, white lights, flashes from bursting anti-aircraft shells. Dirty grey smudges of smoke appeared all around the Stirling ahead which suddenly became clearly visible through the cloud.

The Stirling pilot flew steadily on, mindful of the human cargo he was towing. And then one engine faltered. The blur of the spinning inner propeller on the port side vanished and flame burst in a great bloom through the cowling.

"You okay ahead?" Action Man spoke over

the inter-com. "We see you have fire aboard."

"Don't drop the tow yet," the pilot's voice was terse and urgent. "We've got damage here but nothing too serious. We'll get you over the drop zone."

The flak had diminished, just the occasional stream of tracer shells zipping up through the clouds which had closed in again. The port inner engine on the Stirling was still glowing redly but the fire seemed to be going out.

G.I. Joe glanced at his wristwatch. "Three minutes to target. Heck, I wish we could see something below." He winked at Action Man and added, "I'm telling you buddy-boy, I'd rather be dropping in on the end of a 'chute. This glider job is not my favourite hobby."

"Nor mine. But the top brass wanted to make sure we all landed close together." Action Man's voice tailed off, his concentration upon the 'tug' ahead. Then: "What's he up to? We've been turning off course the last three minutes."

He called the Stirling pilot. "Anything wrong up there? Haven't we reached the drop zone?"

Anti-aircraft fire broke out again all around them, fiercer than before. The gunners below seemed to have found the range. The Horsa began to pitch and roll in the turbulence.

The voice from the Stirling said: "Stand by. We're going lower. Our controls here seem to be broken somewhere. Something's jammed. We may be ten or twelve miles North of the drop zone."

"Ten miles North?" G.I. Joe sounded incredulous. "You know where that'll put us? Over Rachen! Right over the High Street, I shouldn't wonder!"

Action Man eased the controls, keeping in line behind their tug. Rachen was a small German town and well away from the river and twin bridges which was the objective of the airborne assault.

"Can you get us back?" Action Man was worried.

"We don't want to start a one-glider invasion of Germany on our own," grunted G.I. Joe. "Heck, if we don't capture those durned bridges the whole Allied advance will bog down . . . and we will be nicely cut off on the wrong side of the river."

"I'm going to turn right," came the Stirling pilot's voice. "Stand by to follow".

The manoeuvre was never made. The Stirling suddenly burst into flame amidships and the port wing began to crumple. Action Man dropped his hand to the red-handled lever beside him and pulled it back. The tow-rope broke adrift and the Horsa glider seemed to shudder to a halt in mid-air, its speed cut immediately from one hundred and fifty-miles per hour to one hundred.

Action Man put the nose of the glider down, heading through the cloud to an unknown destination below. G.I. Joe turned to the men behind. "Brace up, lads. We're going in."

The burning Stirling had vanished from sight and the glider descended in a shallow dive, cloud zipping past like smoke. It was two minutes past zero-hour for Operation Sky-drop; they should by now have been on the ground and making for the two vital bridges over the river.

At one thousand feet they broke through the cloud cover. Below, spread out for miles, was a sprawling mass of buildings. Tall buildings, churches, rows of residential houses, long-roofed factories with chimneys rising high and connecting streets running in straight lines like the threads of a spider's web! Half the buildings were little more than shells, shattered by bombing raids.

"Rachen!" muttered Action Man, his eyes searching for an open space in which to put down the glider. "Nothing about landing in a town in the training manuals!"

The men sitting in the fuselage had seen from the windows what was below and they didn't like it. But there was nothing they could do except wait. Their fate was now completely in the hands of Action Man.

"Eight hundred feet." G.I. Joe was looking from the altimeter to the ground below. "Running out of height, buddy."

"There's a bit of greenery over there. And water. A lake."

The American turned to look past Action Man on the port side. Coming toward them were trees and past them an area of grass which terminated suddenly before a wide expanse of mirror-like water.

"It's a park!"

"It'll have to do. There's nowhere else." Action Man turned briefly to look back at his passengers. "There's a space coming up, lads. Brace up and think good thoughts. I'm putting her down. When we land . . . everyone out at the double and spread out. We're on our own now."

"Watch it or we'll over-shoot."

Action Man put the nose of the glider down and speed seemed to increase as they lost height. The trees began to look enormous, looming ahead, thick black branches showing menacingly through a thin curtain of spring foliage.

Then they were over the trees and the green of the grass came up to them. The Horsa levelled out and juddered as the huge landing flaps in the wings came down, and cut the air-speed dramatically.

The wheels hit the ground, bounced and Action Man janked the control column back, dumping the glider down hard. Then they were on the ground still going forward. The lake ahead loomed larger, rushing at them. The brakes were full on and the wheels ploughed great furrows. The glider shook and shuddered and finally halted. They were less than ten metres from the water.

G.I. Joe and Action Man slid out of their

safety straps. Now they were on the ground there seemed to be complete silence. It was broken by the sound of the men knocking open the doors and leaping out.

They went out with their Bren guns and Sten guns cocked, fanning out around the glider in a circle. There was little cover but they threw themselves down behind ornamental bushes, squinting down their gun sights, ready, waiting.

Action Man and G.I. Joe snatched up Bren guns and went out with them, running to the edge of the lake, huddling down against the slight slope of the bank, their legs in the water.

Nothing. No movement. No sound.

The lake was three hundred metres across and on the far side partly screened by young trees and bushes was a white-stone building of three storeys. Part of the roof had been shattered by bomb blast and the windows gaped blankly.

"Looks like a hotel or something," observed G.I. Joe. "And empty."

"Let's take it." Action Man glanced at the men from the glider lying around in their defensive positions. "We can't stay out here. We need cover . . . and fast."

Although the Airborne troops were spread out, they were all within ear-shot. Action Man shouted: "You men on the far side, go to the glider and unload. Men on this side follow me when I give the word. We're going to take the white building across the lake." He glanced at

G.I. Joe. "See any movement in there?"

"Nothing. Not a sausage!"

"Then we go." Action Man rose to his feet. "Let's do it, lads. This way".

Fourteen men went with him. The lake bent in the shape of a horseshoe around the white building and they had to skirt it before coming out into a spacious paved courtyard at the front. G.I. Joe's guess about it being an hotel proved correct. The facade was pock-marked with shrapnel and all the windows gaped blankly but huge nail-studded oak doors were closed and above them in large metal letters which were bent and askew was the word KAISERHOF.

To their left, separating the courtyard from the street outside, were tall iron railings. Further, across the street, a long row of solid-looking houses. Immediately opposite the hotel the houses divided to make way for a wide thoroughfare flanked by buildings taller than the hotel itself. The view from the hotel windows would be straight down this wide avenue which seemed to be best part of three hundred metres long.

"Looks like Main Street. Shops, department stores and stuff like that," grunted G.I. Joe. "And all empty. There's something screwy about this town. No one lives here!"

The men with them had taken cover behind a series of ornamental concrete tubs which in happier days had housed flowers but now lay on their sides, spilling dried earth in brown patches on the paving stones.

Action Man beckoned over one of the men. He had flaming red hair and he had lost his helmet. "Stay here and keep me and G.I. Joe covered!" Action Man was staring at the Kaiserhof as he spoke. "I don't think there's anyone inside but if there is, you open up on them when they show."

The man, known as Ginger Collins, raised his thumb in acknowledgement. Action Man tapped G.I. Joe on the shoulder and they rose to their feet and went forward in a fast crouching run. Their rubber-soled boots made no sound. The heart-stopping clatter of small-arms fire which they half-expected never materialised.

At the oak doors they took up position against the wall beside the doors. Action Man put out a hand and depressed one of the two large iron ornamental handles. The door remained shut.

G.I. Joe whispered: "Window?"

Action Man nodded. The windows were too high above the ground for them to climb into and the British Commando said: "You make a back. I'll go in."

G.I. Joe stepped away from the door and crouched beneath the nearest window. Bomb blast had blown out all the glass and frame leaving a gaping hole.

The American signalled he was ready and Action Man ran from the door on to the open courtyard. Then he turned and ran at the window. One bound took him on to G.I. Joe's back and another leap carried him up and through the window. He landed inside on his feet amid a litter of broken glass and debris. The muzzle of his Bren swept around seeking every corner; but the room was empty.

He looked out of the window. G.I. Joe was crouching there and Action Man was looking down the barrel of the American's Bren.

"Good job I know you," grinned G.I. Joe, lowering the muzzle. "If you'd had a Jerry hat on . . . I'd have blown it off. What's it like in there?"

"Empty. Gimme your hand and come on in."

When they were both inside, Action Man went cautiously to the door and peered out into a long corridor with doors leading off at intervals on both sides. Wallpaper on the walls was peeling off and in places the ceiling had split and spilled plaster onto a faded carpet.

They walked down the corridor to a vast circular room. Above, a glass dome shafted weak sunlight through drifting dust. Off to one side a wide corridor led directly to the front door. At intervals around the circle, smaller corridors branched off like spokes from a hub.

"Get the lads in. I'll check around." Action Man pointed his Bren toward the front door. "Usual drill when they get here. Defensive positions. Send someone back to the glider and tell the chaps there to bring in all the supplies . . . and don't hang about."

It didn't take Action Man long to confirm what he suspected. The hotel was abandoned and derelict. All the furniture had been removed and the top floor was complete chaos where the roof had fallen in. Broken glass and plaster were everywhere.

As he came down the stairs the men began entering carrying ammunition boxes. They moved in a quick and orderly fashion, setting up their weapons at the windows, moving in for a long stay. When they spoke, it was in whispers, but they seemed cheerful.

Dusty Miller, the radio-operator set up his equipment under the glass dome.

Action Man nodded approvingly. "Try to contact the people at the drop zone, Dusty. Find out what's going on. Tell them where we are. Ask 'em what they want us to do."

He walked back to the front of the house and entered the first room where he had leaped in through the window. Two men, Arnie Western and Sid Weller stood at the window manning a Bazooka which poked its round snout over the window sill. Beside them were a dozen cases of Bazooka ammunition.

"We put the other Bazooka at the window on the other side of the main doors," said Sid Weller. He jerked his head at the long, wide thoroughfare across the road outside. "We reckoned Jerry might come up there. If he tries it with tanks . . . we've got a pretty good field of fire."

The big British Commando was about to move on when Arnie Western said: "How we off for grub, Action Man? I could do with a bite and a nice cuppa. Anyone brewing up?"

Arnie Western was a big man and well-known for his appetite. In barracks in England he could always be found in the Naafi canteen consuming cakes and cups of tea.

"You'll get your tea." Action Man grinned at him. "Give us a couple of minutes. We won't forget you."

Only two men were assigned to the rear of the hotel, for the horseshoe-shaped lake protected the building on three sides. When an attack came, it would almost certainly have to come from the front. The Kaiserhof was a good place to defend.

* * * * *

When contact was made with the main forces, the news was grim. German opposition had been intense and there had been many more enemy forces awaiting the Airborne assault than they had been led to suspect.

Neither of the two bridges which had been their objective had been captured and the paratroopers were pinned down on the outskirts of the village of Elgorn, on the river bank.

Dusty Miller sitting on an upturned ammunition box with his radio set on the floor in front of him looked gloomily up at Action Man.

"We ain't going to get any help from those guys, they've got their hands full. Sounds to me as though they're up a gum tree!"

"Have you spoken to General Makin yet?"

"No. I'm waiting for him to come through. They were trying to get him to the radio their end."

"When you raise him . . . I'll speak to him. I'll be in the front rooms. Don't leave the set, I'll send someone in here to act as runner for you."

Tea had been brewed and a small soldier with an ugly bruise on his cheek handed a mug to Action Man.

"G.I. Joe's down the end room there," he pointed down a corridor. "Said he'd like a word when you had time."

"Okay. You're Jimmy Green, aren't you? You stay here with Dusty and come and get me when he tells you." The little man nodded and Action Man added: "How'd you get that bruise?"

"Fell over when we landed, didn't I? Bashed me face on the butt of me Bren." He moved confidentially closer to Action Man. "What do you reckon on this place? Bit funny ain't it? Big town like this and no one seen us drop in. Don't seem to be no one around either. No cars in the streets, no people."

Action Man shrugged. "I don't know any more than you, Jimmy, but it's my guess this place, Rachen, has been bombed so hard and so often, the whole town's been evacuated. Could be. Don't forget, the main Allied advance is little more than fifteen miles away."

"Yeah, but they're on the other side of the river!" The little man screwed up his eyes shrewdly. "And they'll stay the other side of the river unless we capture those bridges. How's the paras doing?"

"Early days yet. They'll get the bridges, don't you worry." Action Man didn't want to spread alarm among his stranded forces. It didn't take much working out to imagine what the position would be if the bridges weren't captured. They'd be trapped in Rachen without hope of relief for at least a week, maybe longer . . . depending upon the time it took to cross the river by boat in the face of enemy fire. Given sufficient forces at the river the Germans could delay the advance indefinitely.

G.I. Joe had set up his Bren gun on the last window at the front of the hotel. From there he could fire upon the houses opposite and control the width of the courtyard. He had magazines of Bren ammunition stacked neatly on empty boxes at his elbow.

"What is it, Joe?" asked Action Man squatting beside his friend. "Trouble?"

"Sort of," the American replied lazily. "Guess what was left out of the glider stores?"

Action Man shrugged. There was always something wrong.

"Food," said G.I. Joe. "Should have been

half a dozen cases of ration packs. Enough to keep us going a few days. Well you can forget it, there was only one box. We eat today . . . tomorrow we'll start getting hungry."

"Do the lads know?"

"Not yet. Thought it best to let 'em find out tomorrow." G.I. Joe nodded at the end of the wide thoroughfare across the street. "If we're staying here, maybe it would pay to get out there and take a look around. There are shops out there. Could be tinned grub lying around, they can't have taken everything with 'em."

"Want to try to look?"

"Sure. Nothing else happening right now."

"Wait until I get through on the radio to the drop zone. Then we'll go together."

Jimmy Green poked his head round the door. "General Makin on the radio, Action Man. Dusty Miller says to hurry."

General Makin had lots of news and not much of it was good.

Action Man squatted beside the radio set pressing the headphones to his ears. The General's voice came through loud and clear but every now and then it was drowned out by the sound of thundering explosions and the sharper rattle of machine-gun fire.

"Shall we try to fight our way through to you, sir?" asked Action Man. "We're some ten miles North of your position but we landed okay and the men are fit."

"And you're in Rachen? That's what I got

from your operator."

"That's right, sir. The town seems empty and we've occupied a bombed-out hotel. No opposition."

"You'd never get through to us here and I don't think another twenty-seven men is going to make much difference. The Germans have got tanks here, lots of them and that's something we didn't expect. We're going to keep trying to get through to the bridges but it's doubtful if we'll succeed." The General's voice faded and then he added: "Stand by Action Man, I'll come back to you. Something's happened. Stand by."

Dusty Miller and Jimmy Green stood staring at Action Man. Their faces set in expressions of uncertainty.

"Doesn't sound too hot," muttered Jimmy Green. "General Makin wouldn't speak like that if he thought he had a chance."

"If he and his lads go down, we've had it, too," said Dusty Miller. "Like he said, we'd never fight our way back to the river. Must be thousands of Jerries between us and there."

Action Man wondered what he'd say if he knew they only had sufficient rations for twenty-four hours. It wouldn't improve things.

The headphones began to whine and Action Man clamped them over his ears. It was General Makin and he sounded excited. "We've been interrogating a prisoner and he's come up with some rather surprising information. I don't think he expects us to survive here for long which explains why he wasn't too reluctant to talk.

"They've got a Panzer Division out against us here and they've got another thirty tanks held in reserve to polish us off if needed. The reserve tanks are . . . in Rachen."

"Rachen?" echoed Action Man. "Here?"

"That's right. Now then, if you and your men can knock out those tanks . . . or at least, keep 'em occupied, it could sway the battle here. At least we can keep fighting knowing Jerry isn't going to throw in reinforcements."

"There's no sign of any tanks here, sir. No sign of anyone. The place is deserted."

"Where did you say you were dug in?"

"In an hotel. The Kaiserhof."

"I'll question our prisoner again. Stand by."

For several moments the earphones buzzed with static and then General Makin spoke. "The Kaiserhof is in west Rachen. The tank reserves are grouped on the eastern slopes in a wood just outside the town."

"Can your prisoner tell you why the town is deserted, sir?"

Again a pause and then the General's voice. He sounded very bitter: "They evacuated the entire town three weeks ago. My prisoner says the Germans knew about our coming Airborne attack and moved the civilian population out to make room for their forces. He says the information was passed on by a spy at our

Headquarters." The General gave a short barking laugh. "No wonder we're meeting stiff opposition here. They were waiting for us."

"I'll try to get the reserve tanks tied up, sir," said Action Man. "If they get through to your area . . . it will be because we've had it."

"Good luck, Action Man. Over and out."

Action Man returned the good luck wish but the set at the other end had already been switched off. Action Man hoped it had been deliberate and not due to enemy action. The fighting in the background had sounded very close and fierce.

He handed the earphones and microphone back to Dusty Miller and told him to keep listening. "I'm going to take a look round outside with G.I. Joe," he said. "If I'm not back and there are any more signals from General Makin, pass them on to Ginger Collins, I'll leave him in charge here."

CHAPTER TWO

THE FIGHTING STARTS!

Action Man and G.I. Joe took three others with them. Two tough Scots, Duggie Burns and Ian Roberts and a man from Melbourne in Australia. He had paid his own fare during the early part of the war to bring him to Britain. He'd served first in an infantry regiment and then transferred to the Airborne. Short, stocky and quick-moving he preferred to listen rather than talk but as soon as the fighting started Barry Blane was right in the thick of it.

Action Man and G.I. Joe carried Bren guns and the two Scots took their Stens and spare magazines. Barry Blane carried grenades and a Sten.

They went out of a side door and arrived at the main thoroughfare opposite the hotel by passing through the front door of one of the flanking houses and out through the back.

The tall buildings on the wide street were empty shells. There wasn't a pane of glass in any window and the broad pavements were littered with debris.

They kept off the street, moving through the gaunt, echoing rooms of the department stores. Here and there they spotted dummy figures from tailoring departments lying among the broken beams and scattered bricks.

As they went from store to store, Action Man told them of the conversation he'd had with General Makin . . . and of the thirty reserve Panzers at the eastern end of town.

"There'll be three or four hundred men with the tanks," exclaimed Duggie Burns. "Tank crews, mechanics, recovery vehicles."

"So we keep out of sight," said Action Man grimly. "We've been lucky enough to land here without having been seen. Let's keep it that way. We'll just scout around and see the lie of the land. If they don't look as though they're about to move out we'll wait until dark before we go for them. Then we'll do it in force . . . with all the lads."

As they progressed, they kept their eyes open for food and in the end store they found some. In a sack were some fifty tins of peaches.

"Peaches!" snorted Barry Blane in disgust, peering into the sack which G.I. Joe dragged forward. "Now ain't that just my luck, cobber! I hate the things! Never liked 'em since I was a kid and my old ma served 'em up twice a week for dinner. Forced me to eat 'em, she did. 'Waste not, want not' was her motto!"

"You might grow to like 'em in the next day

or two," smiled Action Man. "It's all there'll be unless we come across something else."

"Won't be for long, Barry. Two days, maybe three at the most, then the Army will be across those bridges and you'll get shunted off back to blighty! Plenty of the old roast beef then."

"Two days will be two days too long for my liking." The Australian dragged the sack into a corner. "Pick this stuff up on our way back."

Inside an hour they'd walked clear across Rachen. On the outskirts there were semi-detached houses with small gardens, similar to the suburbs of any English town of the same size. Some of the houses had suffered bomb damage but not all and Action Man took them in a detour around them. He didn't want to come across a party of Germans on the same foraging patrol they were on.

Now they moved with even greater caution. On rising ground some half mile further on the terrain was heavily wooded and Action Man suspected these were the woods that concealed the German armour.

They took to the open countryside approaching the wooded hill from its eastern side. The massed trees covered a wide area and they reached the edge by crawling along a deep and muddy gulley.

Action Man pointed to the two Scots and Barry Blane. "You wait here. Me and G.I. Joe will go forward. If we're not back in
hour, withdraw back to the Kaiserhof

Ginger Collins. And tell him he's to attack the tanks in this wood as soon as it gets dark." He and G.I. Joe passed over the Bren guns. "We won't need these. This job is silent."

Further into the wood, which consisted of close-growing pine trees, daylight was almost entirely cut out by the roof of foliage. Their feet sunk deeply into the carpet of soft needles and made no sound.

The first indication they had of German presence near them was the smell of a wood fire. The smoke filtered acridly through the trees and as they moved closer they could hear the sound of someone striking metal with metal.

They were flat on their fronts inching their way forward. The ground began to slope away from them and the trees ahead grew more thinly. And they saw the German Panzer camp. The tanks were scattered among the trees with at least ten metres between each one. Off to the right were a collection of recovery vehicles and wheeled repair shops. The metallic banging they'd heard was made by a German soldier, in shirtsleeves, hammering at a spare tank track which he'd draped over the stump of a cut-down tree. Beyond him other soldiers, some stripped to the waist were working on four tanks, busily fixing on new tracks.

Nearly every one of the scattered tanks among the trees had its crew in or around, loading shells aboard.

"The General's prisoner was telling the

truth," murmured G.I. Joe. "This lot are getting ready for action."

"It's up to us to stop 'em."

"How? We can't just take 'em on."

"There's got to be a petrol dump around here. Tanks need petrol and thirty of 'em need a lot of it."

Silently they began to circle the area. They soon found the Panzer camp was contained in a vast hollow among the pines and as they reached the top of the far side, they found the petrol.

Two or three huge lorries sat up to their axles in mud, loaded with thousands of jerry-cans. Behind them, already unloaded and stacked in a heap some ten metres high and thirty metres across were thousands more jerry-cans.

"There's enough there to float a battle-ship," breathed G.I. Joe. "This must be a regular servicing area."

So suddenly that both men started in surprise, a tank engine roared into life close at hand. Then another and another until the trees were trembling under a barrage of sound.

"They're pulling out now!" G.I. Joe looked at Action Man with flinty eyes. "They're gonna get away before we get a chance to have a go at 'em."

"I don't know about that." Action Man gestured at the petrol dump. "I reckon we've got half an hour before they move. It takes time to get this number of vehicles organised and on the road. Maybe we can get to 'em before they clear this hollow. It's just made for what I've got in mind."

"And that is?"

"Drowning 'em in petrol . . . and setting fire to it!"

G.I. Joe let out a long slow whistle. "Yeah. Like it might work. Puncture a few of those jerry-cans. It'll all flow downhill. Yeah, it's got possibilities."

"Then let's do it."

"What about the three lads we left back there?" G.I. Joe grabbed Action Man's sleeve as he started to inch forward. "This is going to take a little time. We've already been gone fifteen minutes. You told 'em to go back after half an hour."

"Let 'em go back. By the time we've done here, Jerry will know he's got some opposition in this area. And if we do our job properly, Ginger Collins won't need to bring the lads down tonight."

G.I. Joe thought it over and then raised his thumb. "Okay, buddy, like you said . . . let's do it!"

There was no guard on the petrol dump. The Germans must have considered themselves secure from attack. Action Man and G.I. Joe moved in among the stacked jerry-cans. Keeping out of sight as much as they could behind the three huge trucks, they began quietly taking off the lids of the cans and tipping them on their sides.

Petrol fumes filled the air. At first the pool they created merely soaked into the loose earth but as they tipped more and more tins over the liquid spread. When it reached the top of the slope it began to flow in a stream down into the hollow.

G.I. Joe began to cough. "Someone's going to smell this stuff sooner or later. They're gonna want to know what's happening up here. We're not getting the stuff flowing fast enough."

The same thought had been worrying Action Man.

"Why don't we just take the brakes off those trucks and let 'em roll down the slope? With luck they'll hit the trees and turn over. That'll release a few gallons."

"They're bogged down in the mud."

"Stick some of these empty cans under the back wheels. It'll give a grip. They'll move okay."

The big British Commando nodded. If the idea worked they'd move more petrol down the slope in five minutes than they could in a whole hour from emptying tins by hand.

First of all they dug down into the mud under the wheels of the trucks, scooping the ooze out with their hands. As soon as they'd made space, they rammed in the empty jerry-cans, kicking them hard under the wheels with their feet. The tanks which were still running their engines below, drowned the sound they made.

The trucks were huge sixteen-wheelers and it took over half an hour before they were satisfied they had a chance of driving them clear.

G.I. Joe swung up into the cab of the first one. The keys were in the ignition and the massive engine started first time. The rear wheels turned, grating on the jerry-cans beneath. Turned and gripped and moved forward. Slowly the giant vehicle dragged itself clear of the huge ruts it was in. And still no one had noticed anything wrong.

At the top of the slope, G.I. Joe pulled on the brake and ran to the next truck. Action Man was already edging the third petrol-carrier forward.

When all three were in position, they went from one to the other, releasing the hand-brakes. The trucks remained where they were.

"Give 'em a shove, it won't take much."

The trucks were already tipped slightly down hill and with Action Man and G.I. Joe straining against the giant wheels, the vehicles moved. Slowly at first then faster, down the slope. They rushed from truck to truck, throwing their weight against the wheels. By the time the first one was halfway down the slope the other two were following it.

At last someone below saw what was happening. There was a single yell of surprise and fear, then a dozen voices joined in.

The three trucks charged on. Now they were unstoppable. The weight of their petrol loads

took them down the slope like a trio of enraged elephants. They bounced and swayed from side to side. Jerry-cans began to fly off in all directions and the first truck teetered violently on to its offside wheels before turning completely over and completing the journey on its side, gouging great ruts in the ground.

The other two trucks, still on their wheels, caught up with it. One ran over the top of it and the other crashed sideways. Petrol from the thousands of punctured jerry-cans flowed in a cascade.

"Get down!"

Action Man grabbed G.I. Joe's arm and pulled the American to the ground. He had seen a lick of flame spurt out from the engine of the first truck to turn over.

Almost before they hit the earth a tremendous flash of fire shot high into the air followed by an explosion and shock-wave which lifted them bodily and crashed them down again. More explosions followed, deafening. A pine tree, lifted out of the ground by its roots sailed through the air and hit the ground not two metres from them, scattering them with earth.

They rose to their knees, peering down into the hollow. They could see at least a dozen tanks among the trees, all of them sitting in a sea of blazing petrol. The trees were alight, flames racing up their trunks to the topmost branches. Where the recovery vehicles and repair shops had been was a scorched and blackened area of bare earth.

And racing up the hill toward them was a tongue of flame . . . the stream of petrol they'd tipped from the jerry-cans in the pile. The fire was racing uphill with terrifying speed.

"Let's get out of here." Action Man and G.I. Joe yelled their intention simultaneously. They knew that when the racing flame reached the dump of jerry-cans, there would be another devastating explosion and they wanted to be as far from it as possible.

They ran with heads down, arms pumping, running blindly from the scene but even so they hardly got clear. The explosion when it came lifted them both off their feet and flung them several metres through the air and it was only the soft carpet of pine needles that saved them as they came down, skidding helplessly over the ground on their backs.

The entire wood now appeared to be on fire. Petrol had been thrown high and in all directions and wherever the liquid splashed so another fire broke out immediately. Dimly they could hear above the roaring of the flames the sound of tank engines and the tinny sound of tank tracks on the move.

The British Commando and the American dusted themselves down, standing unsteadily.

"Sounds like they're trying to salvage what they can," said G.I. Joe. "Asking too much to have got the lot of 'em."

"We did enough damage for two men," said

Action Man with a quick grin. "I don't think the General need bother too much about reinforcements arriving to fight against him. Not for a day or two."

The two Scots and Barry Blane had already left as ordered, and Action Man and G.I. Joe followed, circling the suburban houses again and entering the gutted buildings on the main street. At the far end they could see the Kaiserhof. It looked like home to them.

"They picked up the sack of peaches." G.I. Joe had swung off into the first building, and called after Action Man who was moving ahead. "They're not here now. Shows they got away all right."

Opposite the Kaiserhof they stepped into the street, showing themselves and received an answering wave from one of the windows.

Behind them, in the sky, a great black tower of smoke rose in the air, flattening out as it reached the low clouds and spreading in a dark stain. And the stain was tinged with red, reflecting the fire that still raged beneath.

Ginger Collins opened the big oak doors for them and from the windows arose a cheer from every man watching.

"The lads don't know what you've done yet," Collins greeted them. "But from what they've heard and what they've seen back there," he nodded at the black smoke, "they reckon you've done a fair amount of damage.

"You can say that, chum," said G.I. Joe

modestly. "Did the other three get back okay? With the peaches?"

"Twenty minutes ago." They were following as Collins led them down the wide corridor to the circular domed room. "They brought something else, too," went on Collins. He stopped and made a gesture of introduction. "They got themselves a prisoner . . . top quality."

Facing them across the domed room stood a tall German officer. He was as tall as Action Man and held himself proudly, his blond head erect, his chin jutting. He wore the tabs of a *Sturmbannfuhrer* . . . a Major . . . of the 12th Panzer Division. His uniform was as neatly pressed as though he were about to take part in a ceremonial parade.

Action Man and G.I. Joe looked at each other in astonishment.

"Where'd you pick him up?"

Barry Blane stood against the wall his Sten gun cradled unobtrusively in his arm, but the muzzle never left the German's direction. "Sort of bumped into him as we came back, Action Man. He was taking a stroll through those woods where you left us. Matter of fact, he nearly fell over us. Just had to bring him with us."

Action Man approached the officer and looked into his eyes. He saw no sign of fear there. The man was in control of himself even though he must have been furious at what had happened.

"Who are you? What's your name?"

The German inclined his head. In flawless English he replied. "My name is Otto Hollmann. My rank is Sturmbannfuhrer. My Wehrmacht serial number is 453364."

"What were you doing in those woods? You're a Panzer man. Were you in charge of the tanks there?"

"I am not obliged to tell you anything other than my name, rank and serial number."

Action Man nodded briefly. Looking past Hollman he said: "How long has he been standing here?"

"Ever since he got here. 'Bout half hour . . . three-quarters," replied Barry Blane.

"Get him something to sit on and a cup of tea." Action Man turned to Dusty Miller who sat with his earphones on in front of his radio-set. "Anything more from the D.Z.?"

"Nothing addressed to us. But I've been listening-in to what's going on. Jerry seems to have driven a wedge, dividing our lads into two groups, they're taking a bit of stick."

"Have they got to the bridges?"

Dusty Miller shook his head. "No. I don't reckon they're gonna make it, either."

Blane came back with an empty ammo box and the German officer sat down and took the mug of hot sweet tea that Jimmy Green brought in after. He sipped gratefully.

"When you get a chance, Dusty, call General Makin and tell him we've got some good news.

Tell him he needn't worry too much about Jerry getting reinforced from the tanks in the woods behind Rachen. We've blown maybe half of 'em to pieces!"

Otto Hollmann lowered the cup slowly, his eyes bleak.

"It's true," Action Man told him. "Your Panzers took a bashing."

"I find it difficult to believe," the German answered slowly. "My forces are infinitely superior to yours . . ."

A low growl sounded from Barry Blane.

Otto Hollmann dipped his head fractionally and went on: "Perhaps I should say it another way. My forces are far greater than yours in numbers and fire-power." He gestured around. "From what has been revealed to me here, you are no more than thirty or so infantry men. How would it be possible for you to deal with more than . . ." he checked himself, "with a great number of armoured fighting vehicles?"

"We set fire to 'em, buddy." G.I. Joe was enjoying himself. "We got into your petrol dump and tipped the stuff all over 'em. Three great truck loads and the petrol dump. Went up like a bomb." G.I. Joe examined the nails on his left hand with care, breathing on them and then polishing them against his chest. "An' it wasn't thirty men who did it, my old son . . . it was two. Me and him."

The German bowed his head. When he spoke his voice was thick with emotion. "It is war, I know that . . . but there were many good men . . . good soldiers . . . my men . . ."

'They didn't keep a good look-out," said G.I. Joe bluntly, "or we'd never have got that close."

"Now would you like to tell us a bit more?" said Action Man. "How many tanks did you have before we knocked some out? They were about to move on somewhere. Where?"

"I cannot tell you that."

Otto Hollman looked Action Man squarely in the eye, but his lips were a tight line of obstinacy.

Just what I'd do and say if I were in his place, thought Action Man. And he looks the type who means what he says. He nodded to Barry Blane. "Okay, Blane, there are cellars under this place. Take him down there and lock him up. Stay with him. Don't let him get out."

Blane marched Hollman away and G.I. Joe slapped Action Man on the shoulder. He sounded cheerful and confident. "So all we have to do is wait for the lads to get here. Mission accomplished, eh?"

"I'd like to think so. But we didn't knock out all those tanks, Joe. Maybe we did for a lot of 'em, but it's my bet there's fifteen or twenty maybe, still fit for action. They'll be here soon. They'll track us down in no time."

Dusty Miller looked up sharply, one hand holding his earphones close to his head. His face was pale and he bit his lip. "Jerry's over-run one of our positions at the drop zone. I heard this operator saying just now . . ."

They crowded around the set.

"What did he say, Dusty? What?"

"He just shouted something about three tanks, firing at them, point-blank. And . . . and the lads were trying to hold 'em off with Brens. And then . . . then there was a heck of a bang and the set this end went dead."

Then, almost like an echo of Dusty's words, a shout came from the front of the hotel.

"Tanks! Watch it lads, tanks coming up that wide road . . . three of 'em!"

CHAPTER THREE

THE TANK-BUSTERS!

Sid Weller, squinting along the sight of his Bazooka identified the tanks with one word: "Tigers!"

"The bigger they are, the harder they fall," rejoined Arnie Western with a laugh. "The only thing I don't like about 'em," he added soberly, "is that blooming great eighty-eight gun they've got. Once they know we're here, they're gonna knock this hotel down right around our ears . . . and we won't reach 'em with this." He put his hand on the barrel of the Bazooka. "We'll have to wait until they come through those railings before we've got a chance!"

Action Man and G.I. Joe came in and crouched at the window. The Tiger tanks were still a long way off, at the far end of the street. They were moving very warily, nosing forward and then pausing while their long gun muzzles moved from side to side, searching for an unseen foe.

"Looks like just a general search. They don't

know where we are." G.I. Joe gave a short laugh. "At least we missed three of 'em, Action Man."

"There'll be more than three. And it's no good sitting here at the window and waiting for 'em to knock us over." Action Man patted the two-man Bazooka crew on the shoulder. "I want you two lads to set up shop in that first big building on the corner. You'll be able to hit any tank in that street from there. Take as many shells with you as you can. I'll get some others over to you."

"Now?"

"Yes. But don't be seen. Those Jerries out there are still not sure where we are. Let's keep 'em guessing."

When the two men had left, G.I. Joe shook his head. "Y'know, they're not going to hold off Tiger tanks for long with a Bazooka. It's a good weapon . . . but not good enough."

"What else came out of the glider?"

"Bren ammo, Sten ammo, grenades, Field Service dressings, one case of rations, coupla radio sets, that kind of stuff."

"Any dynamite or plastic explosives?"

"Dunno. I'll ask Charlie Crawford, he supervised the unloading."

Together they went to see Crawford. He was a veteran. He'd been in the Army twelve years and told everyone he'd never really enjoyed himself until he volunteered for the Airborne. "Then I started to see some action," he said, proudly.

"Real fighting, mate. Real soldiering with the best bunch of lads you could ever wish to meet." He was the oldest man in the Kaiserhof.

He said he had two cases of plastic explosives complete with detonators. He showed them where he'd stored them in a cupboard under the stairs.

"Didn't think we'd need 'em, mate," he said apologetically, "not cooped up in here, like."

Action Man filled two battle-packs and handed one to G.I. Joe. "Work to do, Joe."

Once again command of the Kaiserhof garrison passed to Ginger Collins and once again Action Man and G.I. Joe slipped across the road, through the houses opposite, and into the gutted department stores.

Ernie Western and Sid Weller had set up their Bazooka behind a huge block of granite that had fallen across the doorway of the first building. Ernie tapped the block and winked. "Won't be much come through that," he grinned. "We'll be safe as houses."

"Where are the Tigers now?"

"About the centre of the street. They don't know we're here."

G.I. Joe and Action Man moved on. Scrambling over the rubble of the ruined interiors, they passed from building to building. Where there was an alley between buildings they found a side door to pass from one to the other. Just before they reached the position at the street centre where the tanks were, Action Man dropped to his knees by a central supporting wall and attached some of the plastic explosive.

G.I. Joe raised his eyebrows.

"You'll see," grunted Action Man. "Help me with this stuff. I want the central retaining pillars of the outer walls of all the buildings down this side of the street to have a small charge fixed to 'em."

Outside they heard the creaking and squeaking of tank tracks as the Tigers slowly moved on. The black shadow of a turret moved slowly through what once had been a shop window and the long black gun muzzle swung back and forth. They froze, and stood for long minutes until the shadow moved on.

By the time they had reached the far end of the street and fixed their charges to all the buildings, the Tiger tanks were at the end of the street nearest the Kaiserhof.

"Arnie and Sid must have them right on the end of their Bazooka," whispered G.I. Joe.

"They won't fire until we get back. Now, we retrace our steps and stick a detonator in each charge we've placed. Better give it a fifteen minute fuse. We want to be back with Arnie and Sid when it starts going off."

They placed the first few detonators and then stopped. More tanks were coming. Action Man risked a quick look out into the street and pulled his head back hurriedly.

"Stone the crows, this is a bit of luck. There's another three."

"You call that luck? You must be joking."

"They're moving up the street in single file. The first three tanks must have reported it all clear. We'll get the lot of 'em."

They began to work as fast as they could, planting the detonators and then scrambling through the rubble to the next building.

Action Man had timed the operation to a nicety. As they sank down breathlessly beside Arnie Western and Sid Weller, there were two minutes left on Action Man's wristwatch before the first charge was due to explode.

Ten metres from where they lay behind the granite slab, the original three Tiger tanks stood immobile. Their gun turrets were open and the tank commanders were standing up, looking back at the other three Panzers moving slowly toward them.

"What's gonna happen?" asked Arnie Western. "What have you two been up to?"

Action Man motioned to them to duck their heads and held up one hand, five fingers spread. One by one he counted off five seconds. As he mouthed the word 'five', the first charge at the far end of the street went off. And then, one after the other the other charges exploded.

For a split second there was only the sharp sounds of the charges going off and then began a low rumbling sound. It grew louder with every moment until it developed into a crescendo of sound and the ground beneath their feet began to quiver with the impact of falling masonry.

The three Tigers outside began to move. Turret hatches were slammed down and the tracks revolved. The three leading tanks made it out of the street, but those behind had no chance.

The explosive charges placed upon the pillars which held up the gutted shells of the buildings had been blown away and, with no support left, the outside walls of the department stores sagged outwards and fell. Thousands of tons of bricks, girders and rubble smashed down, falling on the tanks in the street, burying them all. And dust rose like thick fog, billowing up, covering the scene in a blinding, choking blanket.

"Great balls of fire! I-I've never seen or heard anything like it." Arnie Western raised his head above the level of the granite block and stared down the length of the street.

Of the three tanks that had been there, not one remained to be seen. Everything was buried under a massive pile of debris which completely filled the street, piling up to the second floor windows of the buildings on the far side. The machines had vanished as though hit by an avalanche.

"Let's get the other three," said Action Man crisply. "Get that Bazooka round to the side window."

The leading three Tiger tanks were now halted in front of the Kaiserhof hotel. Again the commanders were peering from the turret

hatches but they were not looking toward the hotel but back down the dust enshrouded street. They were side on and the range was less than fifty metres.

"Sitting ducks," grunted Sid Weller tersely. "Let's get going, Arnie!"

Their first shell hit the nearest tank amidships and blew its track completely off. The second shell loaded and fired within a second smashed into the turret of the second tank. A machine-gunner in the third tank began to pour bullets toward them in a raking fire that found their window and whined and howled over their heads.

Sid got off another shell just as the bullet knocked him sideways across the room. As he fell the Bazooka went with him and its shell blasted out and whistled harmlessly over the top of the tank.

The turret began to revolve and the monstrous barrel of the eighty-eight mm gun turned slowly toward them depressing to its full extent to get them within its sights.

G.I. Joe hurled himself across the room and pulled the Bazooka from Sid Weller's lifeless hands. "Gimme a shell, Arnie. Load this thing."

Action Man was already at the window, firing his Sten at the oncoming vehicle. He could see his bullets bouncing off the armoured hull without effect.

The eighty-eight fired and its muzzle flash

seemed almost to leap out and touch them, so close was the range. The shell, too high, slammed into the brick work above their window and half the wall fell on them, knocking them to the ground.

They were still struggling to free themselves, expecting to see the mighty tracks of the armoured giant come crushing down on them, when they distinctly heard the sharp crack of another Bazooka firing. Twice, three times in rapid succession.

"It's the guys from the Kaiserhof," yelled G.I. Joe jubilantly. "They've got him."

G.I. Joe was free and he turned to help Action Man push aside a huge beam which had fallen across his legs. Together they struggled to their feet. The Tiger tank was less than two metres from them and burning fiercely, black smoke rising like a funeral pyre.

Action Man winced with the pain from his bruised legs. "Arnie's under this lot, Joe, let's find him."

But when they did find Sid Weller's mate, he was dead, killed by the weight of the masonry on top of him. They salvaged the Bazooka and most of the ammunition and laid it on top of the rubble ready for future use.

"What do you reckon now, Joe?" sighed Action Man. "I don't think they'll risk tanks down this street again, even if they can ride over the top of the rubble. But they sure as heck know we're here."

"They'll put foot troops in," said G.I. Joe with assurance. "They won't like what we've done here. They won't wait too long. They must have a few hundred back there, ready, waiting."

"We want some Brens out here. We'll fight 'em here as long as we can. We'll only pull back into the Kaiserhof if we have to. It's too much of a target. We want to spread out a little."

"I'll stay out here, you go back and check with the General; he'll like to know how we're doing and we've got more good news for him." G.I. Joe slid down behind the Bazooka. "I'll get a few shots off with this if I can . . . Sid and Arnie would like that, I guess."

"I'll send out half our force. You put 'em where you think they'll do most good. See you later."

Action Man set off in a crouching run. This time he went straight for the gate in the iron railings in front of the Kaiserhof. The time for staying hidden had passed.

* * * * *

When men, Brens and ammunition had been despatched to defensive positions among the ruins, Action Man spoke to Dusty Miller who remained at his post with his radio-set.

"Has the General been in touch?"

"Yes, just before you blew up that street over there. I told him you'd duffed up the Panzer reinforcements."

"How's the fighting going their end?"

"General Makin and the men with him are still holding out. But they're pinned down and casualties are heavy."

"The bridges?"

"They're still in German hands."

"What about the main advance? Is the Army coming?"

"They're holding back, waiting for news of the bridges. Guess they don't want to get to the river and find they're stuck on one bank with Jerry on the other taking pot shots at them."

"Okay. I'll be here in the Kaiserhof for a while now. Send Jimmy Green to find me if General Makin gets on the air."

Action Man left the circular room and made his way to the room on the far side of the main doors. The room which housed the second Bazooka crew.

They were jubilant. "Nice shooting, eh, Action Man? We put three shells one after the other right into the turret. Blew it off. Just the right range!"

"If you hadn't, me and G.I. Joe would have had it," Action Man told them. "That Tiger was just about to roll over us."

"What happened to Ernie and Sid? Their Bazooka seize up or something?"

The big British Commando told them what had happened and the delight at their own success instantly vanished.

"Poor ol' Sid. That's tough."

"Arnie, too."

Action Man clapped both men on the shoulder. "Keep your eyes on that street. Maybe you'll get another chance to shoot at something."

He was at the door when one of them called after him. "What about the main assault force? How're they doing? Have they got those bridges?"

Action Man shook his head. "They're getting it tough, too. If you're thinking the Army will be here to take over in a day or so, forget it. It could be twice that long. We've got a fight on our hands."

He had just returned to Dusty Miller in the circular room when Barry Blane appeared in the doorway of the corridor that led down to the cellars. Behind him, grim-faced, stood Otto Hollmann.

Action Man gaped at Blane. There was a cord around his neck and a Mills bomb was tied to it. The grenade hung just below his chin. His hands were behind his back and as Otto Hollmann pushed him further into the room, Action Man saw they were bound with wire. From the pin on the grenade another piece of cord went over Blane's shoulder and was held by the German.

Hollman stood still allowing them to see what he had done.

"He hit me with a brick, Action Man.

Knocked me out."

"And took a grenade," added Hollmann. He held up the cord which was attached to the pin. "As you can see. If anything happens to me and I should . . er . . . fall . . . I cannot help but pull the pin out of the grenade and I'm afraid Private Blane will be the one to suffer. His hands are tied so he'll be unable to help himself."

"What do you want?" Action Man's eyes flashed like fire. "Okay, so you've got Blane. What now?"

"I want to leave. I want to walk from here and back to my men out there," he gestured generally in the direction of the town.

"We could shoot you before you were halfway across the street."

"And if you do, you will undoubtedly kill Private Blane." A faint smile crossed the German's lips. "I don't think you'll do that, Action Man. You're not that sort."

"What happens to Blane if I say yes? How do I know you won't pull the pin in that grenade anyway once you're through my men?"

The Panzer officer shrugged. "I believe you to be an honourable man, Action Man. You must believe the same of me. I give you my word I'll set Blane free, unharmed, once I'm clear."

"Shoot him, Action Man. I'll take my chances!" Blane's face was as white as newly fallen snow, but he meant what he was saying.

Action Man's eyes held Hollmann's for

several seconds but the German returned the gaze unflinchingly.

"Okay, Hollmann, it's a deal. I'll keep my word and I'll expect you to do the same."

Hollmann inclined his head and turned Blane toward the front entrance. If he expected to be shot in the back he did not show it. He marched his prisoner unhesitatingly to the door, opened it and passed through. Action Man followed him.

As the German and Blane set out across the courtyard, the British Commando put his hands to his mouth and yelled: "G.I. Joe. Tell your guys not to make a move. This is serious. Our German prisoner has turned the tables on us. Let him go through unharmed. Blane's with him and he's in trouble. Understand?"

He heard G.I. Joe shout an acknowledgement and Hollmann continued his march forward.

"He'll blow Blane's head off once he's away," grunted Dusty Miller. "He's not going to let him come back to us."

Action Man had returned to the radio room and he said curtly. "Pay attention to the radio, Miller. Give General Makin a call. I want a word with him."

Surprisingly, Miller managed to raise the General at his first attempt. As Action Man donned the earphones he could hear the echoing roar of explosions and the crackle of small arms fire. General Makin sounded very weary.

"You did a good job on those Panzers, Action

Man. But I think we've had it here. The Airborne are prepared to fight to the last man. But the situation is hopeless. I've abandoned all thoughts of taking the bridges. Can't be done."

"Can't the main Army forces help, sir?"

"They're halted five miles on the far side of the river. They've got to wait until the bridges are taken. When I tell 'em we can't do it, they'll have to bring up boats to cross the river . . . and it could be a week before they can find that sort of equipment."

"What about reinforcement? Can't they drop more men in by parachute?"

"Not a chance. Jerry's prepared for them now. They'd be cut to ribbons before they reached the ground."

The General's voice broke off and Action Man's earphones echoed with the sound of the battle raging there. Then: "Jerry's called up the Luftwaffe to finish us off. Half a dozen Stukas are dive-bombing."

"Sounds like Operation Sky-drop . . . is a failure?"

General Makin agreed. "My latest orders are to hold the ground we have. I've replied we can do that for twenty-four hours. By that time the situation may have changed. All we can do now is fight on and hope."

"What about us? We could try to get to you, sir."

"I don't think you could make it. And even if you did, another twenty men or so wouldn't make much difference here. No, you stay put, Action Man. Keep those Panzer reserves away from us, keep them occupied."

Action Man handed the earphones back to Dusty Miller. "Well, Dusty, we stay here."

"How long for?"

"Until we're told to pull out . . . or the Army get through."

A yell sounded at the front of the hotel and Action Man ran to the window.

Barry Blane, the grenade no longer around his neck but with his hands still bound behind his back was making his way as fast as he could toward the front door.

"So Jerry kept his word?" Action Man let the Australian in and began to untie the man's bonds. "Where'd he set you free?"

"Far end of the big street!" Barry Blane's voice was little more than a whisper. "We walked over the top of all that debris. Slipping and sliding all the way . . . I thought Hollman would trip and—and pull the pin out accidentally." Blane leaned against the wall and wiped his handkerchief across his brow. "I don't ever want to take a walk like that again."

"Go and get yourself a cuppa . . . and see everyone else gets a cup, too. Tell Charlie Crawford to brew up and get the food out. It might be our last chance to have a meal in peace."

Action Man didn't know it then, but it was to be their last chance to eat and drink without interruption for a long time. A very long time!

CHAPTER FOUR

THE FIRST ASSAULT!

With the deaths of Sid Weller and Arnie Western, Action Man's force now numbered twenty-five. Just before darkness, the British Commando left Ginger Collins and four men inside the Kaiserhof and took the rest out to the ravaged streets to reinforce G.I. Joe's team.

They set up Bren gun positions and Bazooka crews among the ruined buildings and settled down to wait.

"What's the score at the drop zone?" asked G.I. Joe as Action Man slid down into a hollow among the scattered bricks.

The American was alone, crouched behind a Bren gun sited on a line down the wide devastated main road. A pale moon shone down on the sea of bricks that choked the street . . . and Action Man quietly repeated General Makin's stark account.

"Then we can't expect any help from that quarter. And the Army's holding off, so they ain't gonna be much help to us, either."

Action Man shook his head. "We're on our

own. But don't tell the rest of the chaps. It's better for them to think help's on the way. No point in telling 'em anything different. We'll hold out here as long as we can. As the General said . . . maybe the situation will change."

"It'll change all right," the American grunted realistically. "It'll change for the worse."

Action Man touched G.I. Joe's arm and nodded his head, indicating the street before them. At first G.I. Joe saw nothing. Then several dark shadows moved, flitting across the brick-strewn wilderness, coming towards them. As the shadows came nearer, they took the shape of German infantrymen, the moonlight glinting on coal-scuttle helmets.

G.I. Joe drew back the cocking handle of the Bren and put his cheek against the stock, squinting down the sights. But before he could fire someone else in the small defence force opened up. A long burst that scythed through the advancing Germans.

"Glad to know we're not the only ones awake," G.I. Joe murmured, keeping his eye glued to the sights.

An answering burst echoed from the far end of the street and was taken up by another machine-gun situated in the buildings which still stood on the left-hand side. Another machine-gun joined in until the air above their heads seemed to be alive with whining bullets.

"They've been creeping around for some time

by the sound of things. They've got men all along that side." Action Man risked another glance over the top of the brick barricade, noting the muzzle flashes from the windows of the big buildings.

From across the road, one of Action Man's men yelled: "They're up to something down there. Digging or something."

"Digging?" Action Man and G.I. Joe looked at each other with puzzled expressions. "What do you think?"

"Let's go take a look," said G.I. Joe. "We can move down the right-hand side without too much bother. There's plenty of cover."

They whispered their intentions to the men behind them and then slithered away, moving out of the moonlight and into the dank shadows of the buildings.

Intermittent machine-gun fire from both sides covered any slight sound they might have made. G.I. Joe carried the Bren and Action Man had a Sten gun. Their webbing pouches bulged with spare magazines.

They'd travelled about one-hundred-and-fifty metres when the sound of brick on metal came to their ears. Men were working not fifty metres further on, grunting and straining, tunnelling into the brick-filled street.

Action Man drew G.I. Joe back as far as they could go inside the building where they stood. The entire front of the department store had fallen into the street but above their heads a high ceiling sagged over them. At their backs, a stout inner wall still held a staircase intact.

"They're digging down for the tanks we buried."

"Heck, they won't get them out. It'll take days . . . and a couple of bull-dozers!"

"I think they're just trying to release the tank crews. If they can get the bricks and girders off the top of the turrets, the tank crews can get out . . . those that are still alive."

"And then they'll give 'em fresh tanks . . . or guns, at least . . . and they'll join in the slaughter of our lads!"

Action Man nodded. He tapped his Sten gun and pointed at the street. G.I. Joe raised a thumb, and they took aim. Bren and Sten opened up together. At that range, they couldn't miss and the German working party on the piled bricks melted before the swathing blast like corn before a reaper.

They fired off a complete magazine each and then reloaded, waiting. There was no answering hail of bullets. The Germans in the houses across the street hadn't seen their muzzle flashes and they weren't sure from which direction the devastating stream of fire had come.

Ten minutes passed and then a second working party of German infantry crept out into the street and began pulling the debris aside. They met the same fate as their comrades. The raking fire of Bren and Sten cut down the grey uniformed men before they could race for cover

But this time the German machine-gunners on the far side of the street had been watching and located the tell-tale muzzle flashes.

Bullets cut across the intervening space, smashing into the wall behind G.I. Joe and Action Man and showering them with flakes of plaster.

"Better move back." Action Man made a weaving run along the wall with G.I. Joe at his heels. As they did so, a sub-machine gun ahead of them opened up and bullets spurted the dust at their feet.

"Upstairs! They've got men above us!" Action Man whirled and dived for a doorway. G.I. Joe hurled himself in behind.

"They've cut us off." G.I. Joe eyed the broken, sagging ceiling above. "How many?"

"Can't be more than three or four. But we can't get back to our lads until we've knocked 'em out. They'd get us in the back."

The Germans on the floor above were content to wait until Action Man and G.I. Joe showed themselves.

Action Man gestured at the staircase he'd noticed earlier. "Any chance of going up there after 'em?"

"Don't like it." The American peered more closely. The stairs were fifty metres from them and difficult to see in the gloom. Then G.I. Joe added: "It's not a staircase anyway, it's an escalator. A moving staircase."

"It's not moving now."

"I wouldn't mind betting Jerry's sitting right on top of that, waiting for us to go up."

Out in the street, a third party of Germans had moved out into the street and were again pulling aside the bricks. Even as Action Man and G.I. Joe watched, they saw two of the Germans bend down, half hidden in the hole they'd dug. Then a third German appeared with them . . . a man wearing the helmet of a tank crewman.

"First one out," sniffed G.I. Joe. "And it's gonna be the last." He left the cover of the doorway and slid along with his back to the wall. At the far end, he raised the Bren gun and began firing and on the open street those Germans who were not hit, flung themselves down, seeking the cover of the jumbled debris.

As G.I. Joe stopped firing, the Germans above replied. From his doorway, Action Man caught a glimpse of two men with machine-pistols. They were crouched half-way down the escalator, partly hidden by the balustrade. Further up, almost at the top of the escalator were two more.

"Don't move, Joe," yelled Action Man. "They're on the staircase. They've got a perfect field of fire."

A machine-pistol rattled off its deadly rain of lead and bullets whined and ricocheted around the doorway where Action Man crouched.

"They've got you pinpointed, too, buddy," came G.I. Joe's slow drawl.

Their position was bad. They couldn't break out without being seen by the men on the stairs and if they waited too long, more Germans would be filtered in through the buildings to give cover to the working party in the street . . . until they were hopelessly outnumbered.

G.I. Joe must have been thinking on similar lines. He called: "Is there any back way out of the place where you are, Action Man? I'm hog-tied here. Nowhere to go."

Action Man had already been taking stock of his position. He was in what was little more than a recess in the wall and now as his eyes grew more accustomed to the gloom he could see on the walls, a maze of wires and fuse boxes.

"Hey, Joe, d'you reckon there's any electricity in this place?"

G.I. Joe's voice was incredulous. "Electricity? What the heck are you on about?"

"I was wondering if the power to these buildings was still on."

The Germans on the staircase fired a burst at the doorway where Action Man crouched, chipping the brickwork.

"Think they can understand English?"

"Shouldn't think so. They just don't like the sound of your voice."

Action Man moved the barrel of his Sten gun around the corner of the door and without looking, squeezed the trigger, sending a short burst in the general direction of the stairs.

"Whaddya doing?" G.I. Joe sounded

worried.

"Just giving 'em something to make 'em keep their heads down," Action Man replied. Already he had placed his Sten gun on the floor and was busy with the fuse boxes. The fuses were all intact.

He explored the dim recesses with his fingers, moving from fuse-box along wire conduits until he found another box with a lever in the 'down' position.

"Joe, you still there?"

"Brother, I ain't going anywhere while those four guys are sitting up there waiting to shoot pieces off me," came Joe's voice. "What's with you now?"

"Joe, there's a very slim chance that the electric power here is still on. If it is, I think we can get out of this trap. There's a switch in here and I'm going to throw it into the 'on' position. If the power's on . . . and if it's the switch that sets the escalator moving . . . and I think it might be, we're going to give those four Jerries quite a surprise. We'll bring 'em down to our level."

"You're crazy." G.I. Joe sounded quite happy. "But it's worth a go. Tell me when you're gonna do it."

"On the count of three. If the staircase does start moving, be ready to open up . . . those chaps won't know what the heck's happening." Action Man picked up his Sten in one hand and closed the other over the lever on the wall.

"One . . . two . . . three!"

As the lever went up, there sounded the steady hum of hidden machinery and from the staircase a yell of alarm!

Action Man raised his gun and stepped out of the doorway. The staircase was moving. The steps were moving steadily down and the Germans were in full flight, running hard, trying to run faster than the steps beneath their feet, trying to reach the top.

Action Man and G.I. Joe opened fire simultaneously and all four Nazis fell. One attempted to turn and shoot back but a second blast from Action Man's Sten knocked him off his feet. He gave a cry and dropped, falling across the bodies of his comrades.

G.I. Joe scrambled up to Action Man's side and with guns held ready they stood watching the escalator as it continued to move, bringing down to floor level the bodies of four dead men.

The American let out a low whistle. "I guess they were kinda unlucky. Well, let's move it . . . before our luck runs out, too!"

When the Germans made their next attempt to dig out the buried tank-crews, they had mounted four MG 34 machine-guns on the far side of the road and they kept up a continuous fire on the building opposite. But Action Man and G.I. Joe had gone . . . only the escalator moved.

* * * * *

All night long, the Airborne troops kept up an intermittent fire from their positions at the far end of the street. But by dawn, the Germans had managed to rescue alive eight of the fifteen tank men who had been buried inside their machines.

"I reckon they must have lost just as many as they saved," observed Gordon Hines. He and his pal, Freddie Lane lay full-length behind a barricade of bricks with the barrel of their Bazooka poking over the top. Beside Freddie was a neat pile of twenty Bazooka shells, ready for firing.

They were both grimy with brick-dust and red-eyed from their constant vigil through the night. Neither had slept.

Nor had the men either side of them. To the left, ten metres away, Action Man and G.I. Joe were crouching behind a great iron girder, a Bren peeping over the top. To the right, hidden from view lay sixteen more of their comrades.

For the past half-hour, the Germans had been silent.

G.I. Joe broke the quiet that had lasted between him and Action Man for several minutes. "The boys are gonna need something to drink. Something hot. Reckon we can bring something from the Kaiserhof before it gets too light?"

Action Man nodded agreement. "Tell Wally Scott to call Dusty Miller. Wally's got a walkie-talkie. He's somewhere over that way." Action

Man pointed off to his right. "Charlie Crawford will brew up and bring it across."

Keeping under cover G.I. Joe passed on Action Man's orders and Wally Scott transmitted them to the Kaiserhof.

It was almost daylight now. Action Man had a pair of binoculars and he continually scanned the far end of the street. As far as he could tell, the Germans had pulled out. The street was empty.

As G.I. Joe returned, sliding behind the iron girder in a small cloud of brick-dust, Action Man turned to look back at the Kaiserhof and there, high in the sky above the hotel, he saw six small black specks.

He nudged G.I. Joe. "Reckon they're heading for us, Joe?"

They sat watching as the specks grew larger. They had been in V formation but now they banked and with expert precision took up line ahead. The leader was heading straight at them.

"Stukas!" grunted G.I. Joe.

All the British troops crouched in the ruins had heard the ominous sound of the aircraft engines and every eye was turned to watch the planes. The black cross of the Luftwaffe could clearly be seen.

The nose of the leading aircraft dipped. It seemed to be almost above them. The noise of its engine rose to a scream. One by one the following planes began to dive, plunging down,

becoming larger and larger.

A bomb fell from the leading plane. For a moment it seemed to hang in the air, a black agent of death. The plane pulled out of its dive and roared over the tops of the buildings, at roof-top height. The bomb hit the street a hundred metres beyond the British troops and exploded with a roar that cracked their ear-drums.

Hardly had the first bomb landed than the next Stuka unleashed its deadly load. And the next . . . and the next.

The air was full of noise. The bursting of bombs and the screaming whine of aircraft engines. The already devastated main street of Rachen disappeared in a billowing cloud of dust and smoke. The buildings on the left-hand side which had been almost intact, collapsed as though their very foundations had been snatched from under them.

The iron girder behind which Action Man and G.I. Joe had been taking cover suddenly rose in the air and came down twenty metres from them, whirling like a matchstick in the wind.

And the six Stukas climbed high and regained formation, turning to make a second attack.

"No wonder Jerry pulled out. He'd ordered this air-strike!" yelled G.I. Joe. He turned on his back and raised the Bren, sighting up at the aircraft which were beginning their second dive.

Every man with a Bren gun followed G.I.

Joe's example. Lying on their backs they pumped a hail of bullets up at the diving Stukas. But the screaming engines filled the air, drowning the noise of the Bren guns. The bombs detached themselves from the bellies of the planes and the earth moved and shuddered beneath the exploding bombs. And there was nothing they could do but take it.

Three times the Stukas came in, pounding the British positions without mercy. After their third dive-bombing attack, they soared upwards, regained position in V formation and turned east, flying away.

On the battered street there was almost silence. Here and there a brick fell from one of the few remaining walls and hit the debris beneath, rattling eerily. The dust cloud descended, coating everything and everyone, filling the eyes, nose and mouth with its cloying taste.

Action Man, who had fired off his Sten gun at the diving aircraft, ejected the spent magazine and inserted a fresh one. G.I. Joe did the same with his Bren.

Around them the men were stirring, inspecting their weapons, brushing away the dust on the mechanism. Someone called: "Barney Bates has copped it."

Action Man at a crouch, moved from position to position. Wally Scott lay face downwards, one arm flung out, the hand still grasping his walkie-talkie radio. Action Man could hear

Dusty Miller's voice coming from the set.

Wally was dead and Action Man gently took the walkie-talkie from his hand. Dusty Miller's voice was anxious saying over and over again, "Hallo. Come in. This is Miller. Can you hear me? Hallo, come in. This is Miller, can you hear me?"

"Action Man here, Dusty. Any hits on the Kaiserhof?"

"No we're okay. They weren't after us. What about you? We were watching. Looked as though nothing could survive out there."

"We survived . . . or most of us did," answered Action Man grimly. "We've got some casualties. I'll send 'em back to you. And two dead. Has Charlie made that tea? We could use it."

"He's on his way now. Who — who was it who copped it?"

"Barney Bates and Wally Scott."

"We're down to twenty-three men, then?"

"Any news from General Makin?"

"He didn't call us, but I heard his radio-operator trying to call Army Headquarters. Tried for over an hour but I don't think he got through. At least they're still fighting on."

Action Man said: "Over . . . and out." He switched off the walkie-talkie. Across the road in front of the Kaiserhof, Charlie Crawford was walking. He walked slowly and steadily so as not to spill anything from the two big billy-cans of steaming tea which he carried in either hand.

A thin cheer rose from the bomb-battered men as they saw Charlie.

Charlie had brought with him a dozen tin mugs and he ladled out the tea.

Action Man pointed to four men who were being tended to by their comrades. Two were wounded in the leg and one other had broken ribs. The fourth had a head wound and could barely stand.

"You four go back with Charlie. Tell Ginger Collins to set up a casualty station down in the cellar. Take a breather down there but don't think you're out of it. We're going to need every man who can pull a trigger before we're through here."

When the billy-cans of tea had been emptied, Charlie led the four wounded to the Kaiserhof. The men remaining set to work restoring their scattered defensive barricades.

Action Man raised his binoculars and looked down the broad street. Beyond its mountains of fallen brickwork he saw German troops. They were coming in from the corner at the end and running quickly for the cover of the ruins on either side.

"Stand to, lads," said Action Man quietly. "We've got company. Keep down and don't shoot until I give the word. I reckon we can encourage 'em to get quite near before we let 'em have it."

The Airborne men, still reeling from the dive-bombing attack faced the foe. They were battered, there was no doubt about that but they were a long way from being beaten.

The leading group of Germans had advanced halfway down the street and encouraged by the absence of resistance, were coming on more boldly, forsaking cover in order to move more rapidly.

"They reckon we've had it," breathed G.I. Joe.

"Then they'll soon find out how wrong they are," returned Action Man.

CHAPTER FIVE

ATTACK AFTER ATTACK!

At a range of seventy-five metres, the German infantry became convinced there was no opposition left in the ruins of the bomb-wracked street. In the lead were two men carrying the ugly hoses and nozzles of *flamenwurfers*, containers of inflammable liquid strapped to their backs.

A German sergeant barked an order and the flamenwurfers gushed a jet of flame. It leaped forward in a searing spout, roaring and hissing, burning everything it touched.

Action Man allowed the flame to creep forward another five metres. Then he yelled loudly. "Open fire!"

The men of the Airborne had been lying motionless but now they raised their heads and the blast of a dozen Bren guns and as many Stens, smashed into the ranks of the infantrymen.

Action Man stood up and pulling the pins from grenades with his teeth, hurled them as fast as he could.

The Germans had no time to turn and run. The crossfire of the British guns cut into their ranks, bowling them over, knocking them down. Reducing the advance to shreds.

Those who escaped the bullets were decimated by the fusilade of bursting hand grenades.

The action lasted four minutes and in that time the entire German attack was wiped out.

"Stop firing," called Action Man. He looked at G.I. Joe. "They won't try that again."

"Who do you reckon's in charge of 'em?" asked the American. "That guy we let go . . . Otto Hollmann? He knows how few men we have. He's not going to give up. He's not going to let a handful beat his 'superior forces'."

"It hasn't even started yet," returned Action Man grimly. "Hollman will try to wipe us out. He's got to. If the word got around that one glider of British troops defeated his Panzers . . . he'd get broken back to private and sent out to Russia. No, Hollmann's going to keep after us till he wins."

G.I. Joe looked startled. "You — you think he'll win?"

"Not a hope," grinned Action Man. "Each one of our lads is worth ten Jerries! It evens the odds a bit."

Gordon Hines and Freddie Lane lay beside their Bazooka and re-arranged their stack of shells.

"We're gonna get a chance to use this thing

again in a minute," grunted Freddie Lane. "Can you hear what I can hear?"

Gordon Hines' hand froze on the shell he was lifting into place on top of the stack. "What can you hear, Freddie, my old son? You always did have ears like an elephant!"

"Listen. Just listen!"

They both cocked their heads to one side and unmistakably came the familiar sound of tanks on the move. The clattering and squeaking of metal tracks on hard ground.

"Tanks behind us!" Action Man had heard the noise, too. He cupped his hands to his mouth and yelled: "Bazookas . . . train behind and left. Tanks coming up to the left of the hotel."

There were two of them. They came up the road that ran across the front of the hotel and stopped just out of sight, hidden by a slab of wall on the corner which had not been blown down in the Stuka attack. They were two hundred metres away.

Action Man flipped the 'send' button of the walkie-talkie. "Hallo, Dusty, Action Man. There are tanks in the street in front of the hotel."

Dusty replied: "Yeah. Ginger's seen 'em. He's here now, wants to talk to you. Hang on."

Ginger Collins' voice came through, clear and cool. "There's two of 'em, Action Man. They're not Tigers . . . smaller. Mark Threes, I reckon. Smallish main gun . . . a five centimetre long-barrel and two heavy machine-guns!"

"I don't think they know anyone's left in the hotel," returned Action Man. "Hollmann will have spread the word we were in there but I'm hoping he believes we're all out here now. He'd have got the Stukas to bomb the hotel, too, if he'd thought it worthwhile."

"Sounds reasonable," said Ginger Collins. "What do you want us to do?"

"They'll be watching us. Get out the back door with a Bazooka, Ginger. Bring it round to the front, but keep out of sight. Get as close as you can and blast 'em. Okay?"

"Sounds easy. I'll do that," answered Collins cheerfully. "Over and out."

The two Mark Three tanks didn't come closer. They opened up with their main armament, knocking down the wall that hid them from view with their first shot. The second shell landed well behind the beleaguered troops, the third was short. Then the gunners had the range. Shell after shell ploughed into the rubble sending high fountains of bricks and debris.

Action Man felt a giant blow on the shoulder that sent him sliding sideways across the bricks. G.I. Joe was beside him immediately.

"You okay, buddy?"

"I'm not sure?" Action Man explored his numbed shoulder with the fingers of his other hand. He expected to find blood but his hand came away clean. He moved his arm carefully, flexing the muscles. His arm felt stiff and it ached badly but nothing seemed to be broken. "Must have been a flying brick," he said at last. "Painful but not serious."

Freddie Lane and Gordon Hines wriggled themselves as deeply down into the bricks as they could. Every time a shell landed near them, Freddie Lane put a protective arm over their pile of Bazooka missiles.

"We could rush 'em," he said. "Get to within one hundred metres, then open up on 'em."

Gordon Hines regarded his friend pityingly. "You must be off your nut, mate. What we do is wait for orders. Action Man knows what he's up to. It's not for us to start rushing about and trying to be heroes. You just keep your nut down until you're told to do something else."

Action Man had been keeping watch on the hotel. He'd caught a glimpse of movement on the far side and he estimated Ginger Collins was in position with his Bazooka.

He'd exchanged his Sten for a Bren and now he nudged G.I. Joe and pushed the Bren forward on top of their brick defence-works. G.I. Joe did the same. "Okay, let's keep the Mark Three's attention this way, Joe . . . and give Ginger a chance to get close."

Together they opened fire on the two tanks. They could see their bullets strike sparks as they hit the armoured sides of the fighting vehicles. They immediately drew an answering fire from the machine-gunners inside.

"Don't think anyone will be looking behind

'em out there," murmured Action Man. "Ginger's got it made!"

And at that moment, Ginger Collins, sited no more than fifty metres behind the two Mark Threes, opened fire with his Bazooka. The shells burst against the tracks and then Ginger raised his sights and aimed at the turrets. Shell after shell banged home from point-blank range and at once both tanks stopped firing.

"Jerries coming up the street!" Freddie Lane had turned from the spectacle of the attack on the tanks to reassure himself that his precious pile of Bazooka shells was still there, and as he turned his eyes bulged. Scrambling over the bricks, not more than one hundred metres down the street from which the earlier infantry assault had come, were thirty or forty German infantrymen.

This time they were more cautious. As Freddie spotted them, they dropped down and opened fire from cover.

Action Man and G.I. Joe swung their Brens to meet the new attack. Behind the first wave of Germans, a second wave were advancing, running and stopping, running and stopping. The first wave had now set up machine-gun positions and a storm of flying lead smacked into the barricades of the Airborne men.

Action Man turned to look at the two tanks. Ginger Collins had done his work well. Both vehicles were now burning around the tracks and flames licked up the sides hungrily.

One turret suddenly flung open and the crew began tumbling out, but before they'd gone a few paces, they were cut down by Bren gun fire. The turret of the second tank remained closed and flames enveloped it.

"That's the end of them!" Action Man turned to face the German infantry now securely entrenched less than one hundred metres in front of them. The second wave, one hundred metres behind the first had also taken to cover.

And the Germans in the second wave set up mortars, firing over the heads of their comrades in front, dropping shells on to the Airborne positions.

"Ten minutes of this and we've had it!" Action Man gritted his teeth as a mortar shell smashed down with a tremendous roar not far away. "We've got to sort out those mortars, Joe. Coming?"

"Anything you can do, I can have a go at, too," the American returned cheerfully. "What's the plan?"

"First we get out of here. Second we get around to the side of the mortar crews where we can get a shot at 'em. Got any better ideas?"

"Yeah. I got one better idea. Do you think there's any chance of that Jerry tank back there still being in working order? I mean, do you think the gun will still fire? And I don't mean the tank that's on fire, I mean the other one!"

"They're both on fire!"

"Yeah, but one's just sort of scorched. I don't blame the guys who were in it baling out when they thought she was brewing-up. But maybe they moved too soon?"

Action Man considered briefly. "Look, Joe, we've got to do this thing fast. You try the tank. I'll try to out-flank the mortars. That way we get two cracks at it. Okay?"

"Okay! Then let's go!"

They were both on their feet at the same time. The rest of the Airborne troops opened up with covering fire as G.I. Joe made a dash back towards the silent German tanks. At the same moment, Action Man, firing his Bren from the hip, rushed away to one side, running for the cover of the ruined buildings.

Bullets smacked into the ground at his feet as he ran and he felt a missile pluck at the sleeve of his battle-dress. But he made it. For a moment he paused behind a towering heap of rubble, then plunged on, leaping obstacles, slithering and sliding over loose bricks that moved beneath his feet.

At last he reached a point where he could see the German mortar crews. Like the Airborne troops they had scooped out hollow places in the piled bricks and, kneeling beside their mortars, were firing as fast as they could.

Action Man slammed home a fresh magazine into the Bren and placed four more magazines on the bricks at his elbow. There were three mortar crews and he concentrated upon them

one at a time.

The Bren fired off its magazine of twenty-eight rounds in three short bursts. Each burst cut into the crew of the first mortar like a knife into butter before they knew what was happening.

Action Man reloaded and fired again and the second mortar-crew fell. But by now the supporting infantrymen had located his position and an MG 34 opened up. Bullets smashed into the bricks beside Action Man and his spare Bren magazines went spinning out of reach, slipping down into a crevice between a concrete beam and a smashed water tank.

The third mortar was still firing off shells. Action Man took careful aim but the firing pin hit nothing. The magazine was empty.

He began to wonder how he'd get away. The MG 34 had zeroed in on him and bullets were slapping into the rubble all around him.

It was then that G.I. Joe opened fire from the Panzer Mark Three. As he had suspected, the crew had baled out as soon as they believed their tank to be on fire. But the gun was still serviceable and the fire around the tracks was out. It wasn't quick-firing, for G.I. Joe had to load the gun as well as aim it, a job usually performed by two crew-men. But he managed it and when he did take aim, he did it as carefully as he knew how.

The first shell landed just short of the second line of German troops but it threw up such a cloud of dust and debris that the machine-gunner who was firing at Action Man lost sight of his target. In that split second, Action Man took off, running fast back the way he'd come.

G.I. Joe's second shell landed one metre from the remaining mortar crew and although the crew were merely stunned, the mortar itself was wrecked.

Action Man returned to his own men but instead of settling in with them, he continued his zig-zagging run and reached the tank where G.I. Joe was working busily.

"Want any help?" shouted Action Man down the turret hatch. "How'd you like a loader, old pal?"

"If someone doesn't give me a hand soon, I'm going to fall apart. Come on in."

There were a dozen shells still left in the ammunition racks inside the tank and while Action Man loaded, G.I. Joe aimed and fired. On Action Man's instruction he lowered his sights and began to hit the positions of the first line of Nazi troops. At that range, he couldn't miss, and the Germans began to suffer the terrible pounding that the Airborne had been taking from the mortar fire.

When there was only one shell left in the German tank, the German troops decided they'd had enough. They broke and fled, leaving behind dozens of dead and wounded.

A tremendous cheer broke from the throats of the hardy Airborne men. They shouted and waved in delight and when G.I. Joe and Action Man climbed out of the tank they cheered them every step they took back to the defence perimeter.

But Action Man knew the fight wasn't over.

"We're going to pull back and defend the Kaiserhof," he told them. "We've done all we can here. We can't survive another Stuka attack . . . or a mortaring . . . not out here in the open. Let's get back to the hotel."

For the first time for many hours, there was silence. The Germans seemed stunned by the shelling they'd suffered. Obviously they hadn't expected to come under that type of heavy firing.

But the Airborne men hadn't escaped unscathed. When they retreated to their last defensive positions in the Kaiserhof, only eight of them were not wounded . . . and there were three dead left behind buried beneath the bricks.

As they reached the Kaiserhof, the shadows began to lengthen. They'd fought almost non-stop all day . . . the second day since they'd landed in Rachen . . . most of them had had no sleep and little to eat.

CHAPTER SIX

THE END COMES!

The Germans began their assault on the Kaiserhof just after nightfall. This time they sent Tiger tanks behind the hotel and fired across the lake. Three Tigers with three eighty-eight mm guns pounded the white stone walls of the Kaiserhof to a crumbling ruin.

There was no answer to this bombardment. The range was too great for the Bazookas to be effective and the Airborne men had to grin and bear it.

Action Man sent most of them down to the shelter of the cellars while he and G.I. Joe and Ginger Collins found what cover they could and lay there with their Bren guns, watching the courtyard at the front; it was across this open space that the final charge by infantry would have to come.

"They'll start in when they think we've been softened up enough by the 88's." Action Man glanced at his wristwatch. It showed half-past ten. "They've been pounding us for over an hour. I'll give 'em another half hour . . . then they'll come."

Although the shells from the tanks across the lake hit the hotel at regular intervals, it was surprising how much of it still survived. The exterior wall at the rear and the roof had gone, but such was the maze of corridors and interior walls within the building that the gun-fire was having minimal effect. All the same, everywhere was littered with broken glass and fallen plaster. Here and there a corridor was partially blocked by a fallen girder. The domed roof above the circular room where Dusty Miller had first set up his radio equipment had been blown completely away and the room below was waist high in debris. Dusty's receiver had been hit by falling masonry but the battered set had been evacuated to the cellars where Dusty was trying to repair it.

Charlie Crawford moved among the wounded lying on the cellar floor, bandaging their legs and arms, seeing they were as comfortable as possible. All of them wanted to get back to the action.

"You'll get your chance, mate," growled Charlie to Henry Eastlake, one of the youngest soldiers there. He was barely twenty years old and his left leg had been ripped from thigh to foot by a shell fragment. Charlie had bandaged the limb as best he could but he could see the blood was still seeping through. None of this seemed to deter Eastlake from his appetite for fighting.

"When Action Man wants us up top, you give me a hand up those cellar steps, Charlie. I'm not staying down here. I've won competitions among us lot for the best shot with a Bren . . . I want to get some practice in, okay?"

"Okay," agreed Crawford, moving to the next man. "But you ain't gonna stay down here. There's no chance. I'm getting all you lot up top when the time comes." He said this for the benefit of Alan Morgan as he bent over him. Morgan was mortally injured. Crawford had given the man an injection of morphine to ease the pain, but he was still conscious.

He managed to grin at Charlie. "When you do get me up top, mate, leave me up there . . . the —the air will be fresher. It's stuffy down here . . . can't—can't breathe too well . . ."

"Anything you say, Alan . . . just take it easy. Like a drink?" There was already a shortage of water but Charlie believed a drink would ease the injured man . . . and he wouldn't be alive much longer.

When he'd done his rounds of the injured, Charlie brewed up a pot of tea. Every time a shell struck the building above a cloud of fine cement dust descended and to keep the dust from where he'd built a make-shift kitchen, Charlie had rigged up a tent-like structure with groundsheets.

The men who were not wounded were sitting in another cellar busily filling empty Bren and Sten magazines.

Charlie was passing round mugs of steaming tea and G.I. Joe came clumping hurriedly down the steps.

"Everyone up top. The guns have stopped. Infantry attack coming at the front. Make it snappy . . . and I mean everyone!"

There was a rush for the steps. The wounded came more slowly, limping, helping each other. Charlie kept his promise and aided Henry Eastlake.

Alan Morgan called faintly toG.I. Joe. "Joe, gimme a hand. Can't shift for myself."

The American was well aware of Alan Morgan's condition and he knelt beside the pale-faced soldier. "Better if you stay here, buddy. You've done your share today."

"No . . . no . . . please!" Morgan's fingers plucked at G.I. Joe's sleeve. "Get me up top. I can pull a trigger. I-I'd like to fight it out . . . right to the end." He winced and paused for breath. "The—the Airborne don't give in . . . to —to anyone!"

Somehow G.I. Joe got Morgan up the stairs and through the shell shattered corridors to the front of the hotel. The small force of defenders were waiting, ready, staring into the darkness.

"Get . . . get me to the front somewhere," protested Morgan as G.I. Joe began to ease him down into a protected corner. "Where I can see 'em." His eyelids were heavy with the morphine, but he managed to wink. "Keep me awake, eh?"

G.I. Joe took him forward to one of the shattered windows. When he was seated with his back to a wall, Morgan took the Bren gun G.I. Joe handed to him and rested the barrel on the smashed window-sill. "Thanks! This—this'll do . . . fine . . ."

"What's the matter with you?" asked Action Man when G.I. Joe returned to his side. They were in position either side of the first window past the entrance doors. They both had Bren guns and a pile of spare magazines at their feet.

"I—I was just thinking what a great bunch o' lads we got around us," replied the American shortly. "Couldn't ask for better." He was thinking mostly of Alan Morgan sitting in the lonely darkness, waiting for the attack, wracked with pain, never giving away. G.I. Joe's eye roved over the broken walls around him, through into the next room and the one after, taking in the shadowy forms of the Airborne fighting men, the fit and the wounded.

Suddenly, Action Man stiffened and pointed. On a pre-arranged signal, German infantry came forward from the ruins of the houses opposite. They came at the run, boots clattering on the road. Here and theree a hoarse shout as a sergeant or corporal urged their men on.

For a moment the grey-uniformed horde was halted by the iron railings, but the railings soon collapsed under the combined weight of many men. And as the railings fell, Action Man and his companions opened fire.

The target was too big to miss. The Bren guns scythed through the ranks of German soldiers, tearing great holes in their ranks. But the holes were plugged by more men coming from the rear and still they surged forward.

A stick grenade hurled by one Nazi exploded against the wall beneath the window where Action Man and G.I. Joe were firing, swinging their Brens from side to side, hose-piping lead across the body-littered courtyard.

"They're at the door," yelled G.I. Joe. "And they've got through at the far end."

Charlie Crawford who had allotted himself the window at the far end, because it was nearest the cellar steps, ducked quickly as a grenade hurled through his window and almost hit him in the face. He turned, stooped, picked up the death-dealing missile and flung it from him. It exploded with a shattering roar full in the face of a Nazi who was trying to leap over the window-sill.

The man disappeared abruptly and Charlie emptied his Bren at the oncoming Germans. But there was no holding them. They reached the window and clambered in as Charlie tried desperately to slam home a fresh magazine. As he brought the re-loaded weapon to bear, a rifle butt slammed into the side of his head and he dropped like a log.

Action Man and G.I. Joe abandoned their defence position at the window. Action Man made for the corridor leading to the main entrance and G.I. Joe raced the other way.

The two stout oak doors were splintering under the impact of rifle-butts as Action Man came down the wide corridor. He opened up with the Bren and the battering stopped. He felt someone moving behind him and swung quickly. It was Henry Eastlake. He propped himself against a wall, taking the weight off his injured leg and tucked the butt of his Bren under his arm.

"I can hold this door, Action Man. They need you down the far end. G.I. Joe told me to tell you."

Action Man went past Henry Eastlake on the run, skidding around the corner, almost falling on the broken plaster under foot. As he passed each door along the corridor he was relieved to see men of the Airborne still resolutely holding their positions at the windows, pouring a murderous fire out into the courtyard.

From the end room came the sounds of shouting and scuffling. He paused at the open door, taking in the scene. There were three Germans inside and two more were attempting to climb in the window. In the centre of the room, G.I. Joe was grappling with a huge Nazi sergeant.

Action Man swung his Bren up and let off a burst which cleared the men from the window-sill. The two other Germans, who had been trying to grab hold of G.I. Joe turned upon Action Man, machine-pistols swinging to fire.

Action Man couldn't shoot for fear of hitting

G.I. Joe who was tumbling this way and that as he wrestled his giant opponent. He reversed his Bren, grasping it by the barrel and brought the heavy butt around like an olden-day knight with a two-handed sword.

The force with which he caught the nearest German sent a jarring shudder up his arms. The second German got in a burst of fire and the muzzle flashes seemed to burn Action Man's face; but miraculously the bullets passed over his head and before the man could fire again, the Bren butt swung into the side of his face and he fell.

Another Nazi appeared at the window but by now Action Man had the Bren the right-way round and a burst of fire removed the invader.

Suddenly G.I. Joe fell backwards but he had hold of the lapels of the towering German NCO, and the man fell with the American. Up came G.I. Joe's feet into the man's midriff and as they hit the floor together, the German sailed over G.I. Joe's body and smashed into the wall with a force that shook the room. The body, limp as a rag doll, slid down the wall and sudsided in a silent heap.

Action Man, now crouched at the window, fired off a long burst without looking round, but there was a grin on his face.

"Can't leave you for five seconds without you getting into trouble, can I?" He aimed another burst at two Germans making a determined run toward him and they both skidded sideways and dropped.

G.I. Joe had picked up a Bren and was checking the magazine to make sure it was full. He slid the barrel over the window-sill and snorted.

"Listen, man, if I hadn't come down here, this place would be swarming with Jerries by now. They were inside, I tell you."

"There's three still in here." Action Man glanced at the unconscious bodies lying behind them. "They may be dead, but we don't want 'em here. Gimme a hand and shove 'em out."

They dropped the three Germans out through the window. The attack seemed to be petering out. There were still Germans in the courtyard but they were firing from a prone position; the rush to take the hotel had been halted.

A groaning sound made them turn. Charlie Crawford, half hidden under a mass of plaster that had fallen from the ceiling, was raising himself on hands and knees. The side of his face was a mass of blue-black bruise and dried blood.

"Man, what hit you?" G.I. Joe dropped to his knees and looked at Crawford's injured cheek. "You'd better get that cleaned up, Charlie. You okay, otherwise?"

Crawford hauled himself to his feet and stood swaying uncertainly. He put his hand gingerly to his cheek and grimaced.

"Forgot to duck," he muttered wryly. "Thanks for helping out here." He pulled a field dressing pack from his pocket and began to unwrap the bandage it contained. "Okay, I can look after this window now." He peered out into the courtyard which was littered with the bodies of fallen Germans. "They're pulling back, anyway."

It was true. The first assault on the Kaiserhof had been held. The Germans who could still move were retreating to the cover of the ruins across the road. The fighting, bitter and relentless, had lasted two hours.

* * * * *

At three-o-clock the Germans mounted their second attack. They pushed it forward regardless of their losses for an hour and a half before finding themselves forced to fall back.

And they came again just before dawn. But the men of the Airborne held their positions and fought off the third assault. As daylight revealed the wreckage of the Kaiserhof, the defenders looked around in awe.

The courtyard was a graveyard of German troops. Hundreds of bodies lay around covering the paving from the broken railings to the very windows of the building; and beneath the windows they were piled three and four deep.

Somewhere among the ruined hotel a fire was burning and smoke rose slowly above the heads of the defenders, bowed now with weariness.

Alan Morgan was dead. He still sat with his back against the wall and the Bren gun lay at his side. There were ten empty Bren magazines strewn around his feet.

Harry Eastlake was dead, too. He had been shot while holding the front doors. The splintered oak had been forced back and on the steps outside the German attackers lay where they'd fallen, defeated by the resistance of the wounded Britisher.

Ginger Collins had his arm in a sling, supporting a broken wrist. He, Action Man and G.I. Joe leaned wearily on their window-sill surveying the scene. Action Man had two livid grazes running from one side of his forehead to the other. That was how near the German machine-pistol bullets had come to ending his life in the hand-to-hand action.

"I've just checked around," Action Man said slowly. "We're down to twenty-one men." He looked up sideways at G.I. Joe. "You're the only one who isn't wounded. You and me, that is,"

"How bad are the others?"

"Three are serious. They're unconscious and will have to stay down in the cellar. Most of the others have been wounded more than once. I've ordered the worst of 'em down there and Charlie Crawford's making a meal for everyone. Half a peach each!"

"So there's only eighteen of us left to face the next attack?"

"That's right. You stay here with Ginger, Joe. I want to find out if Dusty's got anything more from the drop zone. If Jerry starts up again, open fire . . . we'll all be up within seconds."

Dusty's news was grim. The last contact he'd had with General Makin had relayed the message that Makin intended to fight on with his men. There'd be no surrender. It was hoped they'd be able to make another broadcast but the radio batteries were running out and they'd been unable to find spares.

"Did he say anything about us?" asked Action Man.

Dusty shook his head. "No."

At mid-day, the alarm was raised as the Germans made another frontal assault across the courtyard. The wounded were carried and helped to walk from the cellars and placed in positions where they could shoot.

"How's the ammunition position, Joe?" Action Man had asked G.I. Joe to check their stores just before the attack began. "Is there enough for another few days of this?"

"Few days? You must be joking!" G.I. Joe sounded aghast. "There's only a handful of us. There's still hundreds of Germans out there. We're not going to hold 'em off for ever."

"We can try."

"And we're nearly outa food. And water."

"There's a lakeful of water behind us. So long as we can light a fire and boil it before we use it, it should be all right."

"Whatdda we do for grub? Charlie Crawford

thinks there's enough for one small meal each. He suggested we ought to let the chaps eat what's left this evening. After that . . ." G.I. Joe shrugged his shoulders. "Heck, how long can the boys hang on? It'll be four days! Four days with hardly any sleep, not much grub . . . and fighting. How much longer can they go on?"

Action Man hesitated before he answered. Then he said quietly: "They can go on for ever, Joe. You ask 'em . . . there won't be a man who'll talk of surrender. They're the Airborne."

This time the German attack was half-hearted. They seemed content to hurl grenades which exploded short of the windows and to keep up a sniping fire, which although it kept the defenders at their positions, was more of a nuisance than a dangerous threat.

Then three Germans emerged from the wrecked buildings. One of them carried a white flag fastened to the end of a rifle which he held aloft.

Action Man called for a cease-fire and his companions lowered their weapons, watching the three men advance uneasily, suspecting a trick.

G.I. Joe was squinting down the sights of his Bren gun, the barrel tracking the movements of the approaching enemy.

"If they try sum'p . . . they ain't gonna live to laugh about it."

"It's Otto Hollmann!" exclaimed Action

Man.

The Sturmbannfuhrer came to a halt in the centre of the courtyard, flanked by two junior officers. His uniform was as neatly pressed and correct as it had been the first time Action Man had seen him. This time he wore a peaked cap which concealed his blond hair.

The tired British troops watched and waited.

"Is Action Man there?" The German's voice echoed around the courtyard coldly. "If—if he has been killed . . . or wounded, perhaps I could speak to the man now in charge. There will be no shooting from my men while we speak, I assure you."

"I'm alive and well, thanks, Hollmann!"

The German's attitude seemed to relax slightly. He gave a small bow. "I'm pleased to hear that. Shall we talk?"

"What about?"

Otto Hollmann spread both arms in a gesture, a gesture that took in the litter of bodies in the courtyard and the battered ruins that concealed the British troops."

"I am asking you to surrender. Your position is hopeless. You must know that for yourselves. I can also tell you that General Makin's men have been overrun. The survivors are now on their way to prisoner-of-war camps. You can expect no help from that quarter. Surrender, Action Man. You and your soldiers have fought well and valiantly . . . you have given everything a soldier can be expected to give."

The Airborne men listened silently. They sat in their cramped defence posts, red-eyed from lack of sleep, dirty, unshaven, wounded and desperately tired.

"What do you say, lads?" Action Man left the window and clambered through the shattered rooms. "What do you say? Do we give in? Or do we fight? Like the man said . . . you've done all that can be expected from a soldier! There'd be no disgrace."

"I ain't giving in to no-one!" shouted someone hoarsely and defiantly. "Heck, I like it here!"

"We don't give in." The cry was taken up by one man after another. And then someone yelled: "We're the Airborne. Tell him that, Action Man. We're the Airborne!"

Above the smoking ruins, rising from the Kaiserhof Hotel which resembled nothing more than a pile of wreckage, rose the shout: "We're the Airborne!"

Action Man returned to the window. "You heard, Hollmann. You're not fighting ordinary soldiers."

"You are the Airborne." Hollmann spoke the words so softly that Action Man wondered if they had been meant to be heard. "So!" Hollmann took a step forward and swept a hand around at the bodies sprawled everywhere. "We fight on. Firstly, may I take away the dead here and give them a decent burial? If you have men to bury, Action Man, you could use the time, too."

"We've already taken care of that," the big Britisher replied tersely. "I'll give you twenty minutes to clear your dead. Twenty minutes. After that we start shooting."

Otto Hollmann hesitated a second and then turned on his heel and strode away. Action Man heard him shouting orders and waiting stretcher-bearers ran forward and began their grim work.

Action Man descended into the cellar. Crawford was busy as ever, making tea.

"Got the last of the grub ready, Charlie? We'll have it now. There's a twenty minute truce before we go at it again. Get it up here to the lads . . . and the tea."

"After that?" asked Charlie, the ugly bruise on his cheek had hardened into a huge black lump.

"After that, we'll see what happens."

Action Man turned away and entered the cellar where Dusty Miller's radio set was situated. The battered receiver, repaired by the little man, stood on an upturned ammunition box, an aerial trailing up the stairs into the open.

Action Man switched on the transmitter and reached for the earphones and mike.

"Action Man calling. Action Man calling. If you can hear me, come in. Anyone . . . come in. Over."

Ten minutes passed as he repeated and

repeated his call and he was about to take off the headphones when there came a rush of static and a very faint voice. "This is Donkey Seven. Donkey Seven at Army H.Q. I hear you faintly, Action Man. Over."

Action Man asked for news of General Makin and was told that the General's forces had been overrun, although fighting was still going on.

"How much longer can you hold your position at Rachen?"

"I don't know."

"The main advance may reach you soon. The Army is going to attempt a crossing of the river by boat tonight. We could be with you within twenty-four hours."

"I hope so," responded Action Man laconically. "Make it soon or we might not be here."

The operator said 'good luck' and the set went dead.

He told G.I. Joe what he had heard. "General Makin's men never captured the bridges! Well, maybe the Army can cross by boat. I'll tell the lads, okay?"

Action Man agreed and as the news spread, new life rippled through the almost exhausted men. There was hope. They drank Charlie Crawford's tea and ate their last mouthful of food. Maybe their next meal would come from an Army kitchen. Good hot tasty food and after, sleep in a comfortable billet.

As soon as the courtyard was cleared the

Tiger tanks behind the lake began to lay down a pattern of fire on the ruins of the Kaiserhof, systematically raking it from end to end and back.

The men of the Airborne retired to the cellars to wait out the barrage.

Dusty Miller, on Action Man's orders made repeated attempts to establish radio contact with the Army again without success.

The cellars shuddered and shook under the weight of the shelling and sleep was impossible. In the light of the stunted candles which was all they had left, the grey faces of the men were anxious.

"Can we do anything about those tanks?" shouted G.I. Joe, yelling to make himself heard above the continuous roar of explosions. "They've got it too much their own way."

"I've been thinking on those lines. How about you and me swimming across the lake when it's dark. Say in an hour's time. We could make a raft, load it with grenades. I'll bet those tanks are firing with their turrets open."

"They sure won't be expecting trouble from us." G.I. Joe sounded excited. "Heck, let's give it a go, Action Man. It's gotta be me and you, the rest of these guys ain't fit enough."

Making a raft was no problem. The hotel was littered with planking that had fallen from the upstairs floors and there were enough bent nails to weld the planks into a stout platform.

When it was dark, they carried the raft from

the ruins to the water's edge and floated it on the lake. On top they placed two Bren guns, spare magazines and a dozen grenades. Every two seconds the lake was lit with the reflection of a muzzle flash from the tanks.

A shell fell short and hit the edge of the lake, covering them in mud and water.

Ginger Collins had come to the water's edge to help them and as they waded out, pushing the raft, he gave them the thumbs-up sign. "You get rid of those babies over there . . . and the boys'll hold out here for ever," he promised them. "All the best."

The water was cold. It bit into their bones and the swim across seemed endless. Every moment they expected to hear the staccato fire of a machine-gun as the tank crews saw them coming.

But they made it. They had veered away at an angle so that they would reach the further side some distance from the tanks.

After pulling the raft up the bank, they took their Bren and grenades and slipped silently across the grass, using what cover they could find from the scattered ornamental bushes. When they reached a position some thirty metres behind the Tiger tanks, they lay motionless on the damp grass, watching.

The tanks stood together in line abreast and fired alternately. First the far left then the centre and then the right. Each shot lit up the area for a split second and Action Man and G.I.

Joe could see several members of each tank crew standing around outside the tanks. Apparently, only the gunner and loader were inside.

It would be hot inside the tanks, firing a barrage . . . and the hatches on top of the gun turrets were open.

"How do we handle it?" G.I. Joe looked enquiringly at Action Man. "One of us opens up on the men outside the tanks and the other gets close and lobs in the grenades?"

"That's the best way." Action Man passed his Bren across to G.I. Joe and then the spare magazines. "Move in a little nearer . . . not too close. I'll go wide and come in from the side. Give me . . . four minutes to get in position and then open up. Keep firing. Don't give 'em a chance to get back in the tanks. And keep the aim low or you're gonna knock me off as I climb on the tanks."

"Now what would I do a thing like that for?" G.I. Joe grinned broadly. "Okay. The plan's good. Let's do it!"

They split up and Action Man vanished into the gloom. He moved swiftly and silently, running a few yards and then dropping down, crawling on and rising to his feet to run again. If anyone among the tank crews caught a glimpse of him, they wouldn't be sure what it was they had seen.

At the end of four minutes he was less than five metres from the left-hand tank. The tank guns were still firing steadily and deliberately at their stationary target across the lake. The tank crews not involved had formed a group at one side and were smoking and talking without thought of danger. No answering shot had come their way from the hotel and they were not expecting trouble.

G.I. Joe gave Action Man four-and-a-half minutes to make sure the Britisher was ready. For several seconds he had been lying behind his Bren gun, looking down the sights at the bunched tank men. He took a deep breath and slowly squeezed the trigger. The Bren thudded against his cheek and shoulder and a deadly stream of bullets hit their target.

As soon as he heard the Bren firing, Action Man leaped to his feet and ran at the nearest tank. One bound took him onto the tracks and another brought him up against the turret. He'd already pulled the pins on two grenades and, opening his fingers to allow the handle to fly off, he dropped them through the hatch and pushed the lid down.

Then down and up on to the second tank. Two more grenades went inside. From the first tank came muffled explosions. As he leaped down and headed for the third tank, one of the crewmen who had escaped the deadly fire from G.I. Joe came up from the ground where he had hurled himself. In his hand he held a Luger pistol.

Action Man ignored the Luger. He slid sideways and skidded around the front of the tank, pulling the pins from his last two grenades. The German ran after him.

Inside the tank the gunner fired off another round and the long barrel of the eighty-eight mm gun above Action Man's head belched flame and fire. And it saved his life. The man with the Luger had chased after Action Man and as the British Commando scrambled up on to the tank hull, he raised the pistol in both hands, at point-blank range. That was the moment the gun fired 'and the searing muzzle flash blinded him temporarily. The Luger bullet hit Action Man high on the shoulder and almost knocked him over. But he clung on to the hatch and dropped his grenades inside . . . leaning against the lid to force it down.

The man with the Luger was reeling around beneath the tank's gun barrel, waiting for his vision to clear. Action Man launched himself feet first off the tank's hull and his boots crashed into the German's midriff. In an instant, Action Man was on his feet. He saw the Luger lying on the grass and kicked it metres away. The German, winded, lay on his side, both hands holding his middle, gasping for air.

The man wasn't going to give any trouble and Action Man turned and ran toward the place where he and G.I. Joe had left the raft. As he ran, the third tank erupted as the grenades exploded inside. The whole action from first to last had taken a few minutes, and three great tanks sat like stranded whales, their insides blown to pieces.

G.I. Joe wasn't at the raft when Action Man reached the lake's edge but he appeared within seconds. He was hobbling and grimacing in pain.

"They took a coupla shots back at me. Took a bullet in the leg. I don't think it's all that bad . . . but it sure as heck hurts."

He noticed the stain on Action Man's tunic shoulder. "They got you, too?"

"And it sure as heck hurts," echoed Action Man, but he managed a grin. "Come on let's get this raft in the water before we both start crying."

The swim back took them a lot longer than the passage out. Both wounded men were feeling the effects of their injuries but they clung on to the raft and moved their arms and legs as best they could. And they reached the rear of the Kaiserhof Hotel.

Charlie Crawford examined them critically as he had every other member of the small force. He bandaged their wounds. "It's just as well you two copped a packet," he told them seriously. "Wouldn't look good when we get outa here, would it? You two the only ones not hurt. People might believe you'd been keeping your nuts down and letting everyone else take the risks!"

"You got any more jokes like that?" G.I. Joe hobbled to the far side of the cellar and sank down between two more bandaged men. "We put those tanks outa action so's we could all get some shut-eye. That's what I'm gonna do right now."

Action Man, too, slumped down against the wall and closed his eyes.

"Me and Ginger Collins are staying awake," called Charlie Crawford softly. "Ginger's up top with Dusty Miller, keeping watch. You sleep . . . you've earned it."

* * * * *

It was one o'clock when Action Man and G.I. Joe made their way back across the lake. At half-past four, all the men sleeping fitfully in the cellars were jerked awake by the deafening explosion of an eighty-eight mm shell exploding above their heads. It was followed by another . . . and another. The barrage was back. Otto Hollmann had moved in three more Tiger tanks on the far side of the lake and with them he sent thirty infantrymen. A similar operation against the tanks would have no chance.

* * * * *

Throughout the fifth day of the defence of the Kaiserhof Hotel, the men of the Airborne fought off repeated German attacks across the courtyard. Twice the Nazi forces managed to get inside the ruined hotel and twice they were thrown out in bitter hand-to-hand fighting.

During the night, the barrage from the tanks continued. Not quite so intense as before but the shelling was regular enough to destroy all sleep.

Action Man and G.I. Joe were keeping watch at the front of the hotel. There were no windows left, and not very much of the outer wall. All had been blasted into a mass of rubble. But they huddled among the tangle of bricks, using the debris as a barricade.

"The Army should have been here yesterday," said G.I. Joe. His cheeks were covered with stubble and his eyes, sunken, looked dazedly at Action Man. "I don't reckon they're coming."

Action Man was in no better state than his friend. He could barely move his injured arm and he, too, had a growth of beard that made him look like a hollow-eyed convict on the run.

"I think you're right. It's the river. They can't get across and Jerry's entrenched on this side now. If only we'd captured those bridges. The whole thing would have been simple."

"They were waiting for us. Our boys had no chance. Someone spilled the beans."

"Think General Makin and his chaps are still fighting on?"

"Yeah, I do." Action Man turned slowly to ease his aching arm. "They're the same as we are. They wouldn't give in. Fight till they drop. Best fighting men in the world!"

"The American Rangers ain't so bad . . . or the Marines."

"Top men!" agreed Action Man. "Wish a coupla hundred of 'em would turn up right now."

There was a movement behind them and Dusty Miller crawled toward them. He had broken a leg in a fall the day before but Charlie Crawford had set it in splints and the little man could just about get around.

"I've just been talking to the Army, Action Man. General Makin's been relieved. They've taken him back over the river.

Action Man and G.I. Joe gaped at Miller. "You — you've spoken to the Army? They've got the General?"

"They brought in supplies . . . everything."

"You mean . . . the Army are across the river?" G.I. Joe couldn't believe it. "They've crossed the river?"

"Be here round about noon."

"Wow!" Action Man and G.I. Joe sank back against the piled bricks. They turned their heads to smile at each other. "We made it, old buddy-pal," muttered G.I. Joe. "We made it!"

"Have you told the others?"

Dusty nodded. "Yeah. They — they were sort of too tired to say much."

* * * * *

At daylight, Sturmbannfuhrer Otto Hollmann entered the courtyard under a white flag of truce carried by one of his aides.

The men of the Airborne, out from the cellars now the tank bombardment had ceased, watched him silently over the barrels of their guns. Behind Hollmann, drawn up on the road, were seven tanks and a long line of trucks and transports.

"Far enough, Hollmann!" shouted Action Man as the German officer reached the centre of the courtyard. "What is it this time?"

"Your Army have crossed the river in strength during the night. Within hours their advance units will reach Rachen."

"So?"

"How many men do you have alive, Action Man?"

"Enough to fight you off if you feel like starting up again. Tell me, Hollmann . . . how many tanks do you have left?"

"I doubt if you have more than twenty men in there with you," the German went on, not making a reply to Action's Man's jibe. "All of them must be wounded."

"We can still fight."

Hollmann drew himself up to his full height. "I have no doubt of that. I am disengaging, Action Man. I have received orders to take up new defence positions further east. Before I go I wish to congratulate you upon your defence of this heap of ruins. You have fought gallantly."

He stepped forward one pace and his hand

rose to the peak of his cap in a military salute. "I shall remember you . . . the Airborne! Good luck."

Otto Hollmann turned briskly upon his heel and marched away. They watched him board the leading tank and the white flag was thrown to the ground. Then the tanks moved forward and the line of trucks and other vehicles followed. Within three minutes the rattle and clatter of the tank tracks had disappeared from earshot.

The men of the Airborne watched the disappearance of their enemy without word. They could hardly believe what they saw.

* * * * *

When the Army arrived at the Kaiserhof, they were led by a young Captain riding in a Jeep. It swung into the courtyard and slid to a stop in front of the ruined Kaiserhof.

"Anyone there?" he called. "The Army's here!"

The small band of men, all of them wounded, supporting each other, staggered from the debris. They could never look smart in their torn and tattered uniforms; with their grimy bandages and red-rimmed eyes. But they still carried their weapons.

Eighteen men of the Airborne formed up into two lines and came to attention as well as they could. Action Man stepped forward and slowly brought his injured arm up in a formal salute.

"Pleased to see you, Captain," he croaked. "If you'll take the Kaiserhof Hotel from us . . . we'll hand it over and fall out!"

THE END

OTHER EXCITING ACTION MAN ADVENTURE STORIES NOW AVAILABLE AS CORGI-CAROUSEL PAPERBACKS

HOLD THE BRIDGE

The Bridge at Breve had to be captured from the Germans and kept open. With only a handful of men, Action Man knew that the chances of taking the bridge were remote — but they had to try. And then Action Man met G.I. Joe and the odds swung a little in their favour . . .

SNOW, ICE AND BULLETS

Trapped in Norway by the German invasion, Professor Lindfors, a brilliant scientist, was desperate to escape and work to free his country.
Action Man and G.I. Joe had a top-secret mission — to get the Professor back to England. On reaching Norway, they found that the Germans were one step ahead of them — Professor Lindfors had been taken to the impregnable prison at Castle Richbleau . . .

THE TAKING OF MONTE CARRILLO

Inside the hill known as Monte Carrillo, the Germans had set up an intricate communications system. Nothing could move on the surrounding plain without being seen and blown to pieces.

Trapped in a bombed-out village with a handful of men, Action Man and G.I. Joe knew that Monte Carrillo had to be put out of action. It was an impossible mission — but they had to achieve the impossible . . .

TO BE PUBLISHED IN NOVEMBER 1977

Two more ACTION MAN Adventure Stories
by the same author

THE TOUGH WAY OUT

COUNTER-ATTACK

Both at 50p

CORGI CAROUSEL BOOKS LTD

A DIVISION OF TRANSWORLD PUBLISHERS LTD

If you would like to receive a newsletter telling you about our new children's books, fill in the coupon with your name and address and send it to:

Gillian Osband,
Transworld Publishers Ltd,
Century House,
61-63 Uxbridge Road, Ealing,
London, W5 5SA

Name ....

Address ....

....

....

CHILDREN'S NEWSLETTER

All the books on the previous pages are available at your bookshop or can be ordered direct from Transworld Publishers Ltd., Cash Sales Dept., P.O. Box 11, Falmouth, Cornwall.

Please send full name and address together with cheque or postal order — no currency, and allow 10p per book to cover postage and packing (plus 5p each for additional copies).